STEM ADVENTURES

THE **AMAZING STORY** OF
CELL PHONE TECHNOLOGY

MAX AXIOM
STEM ADVENTURES

by Tammy Enz

illustrated by Pop Art Properties

Consultant:
Akbar M. Sayeed, PhD
Professor
Department of Electrical and Computer Engineering
College of Engineering
University of Wisconsin-Madison

CAPSTONE PRESS
a capstone imprint

Graphic Library is published by Capstone Press,
1710 Roe Crest Drive, North Mankato, Minnesota 56003
www.capstonepub.com

Library of Congress Cataloging-in-Publication Data
Enz, Tammy.
  The amazing story of cell phone technology : Max Axiom STEM adventures / by Tammy Enz ; illustrated by Pop Art Properties.
      pages cm.—(Graphic library. STEM adventures.)
  Summary: "In graphic novel format, follows Max Axiom as he explains how cell phones work"—Provided by publisher.
  Audience: Grade 4 to 6.
  Includes bibliographical references and index.
  ISBN 978-1-4765-0137-6 (library binding)
  ISBN 978-1-4765-3457-2 (paperback)
  ISBN 978-1-4765-3453-4 (eBook PDF)
  1. Cell phones—Juvenile literature. 2. Cell phones—History—Juvenile literature. 3. Cell phones—Comic books, strips, etc. 4. Cell phones—History—Comic books, strips, etc. 5. Graphic novels. I. Pop Art Properties, illustrator. II. Title.
  TK6564.4.C4E59 2014
  621.3845'6—dc23   2013003113

Designer
Ted Williams

Cover Artist
Marcelo Baez

Production Specialist
Eric Manske

Editor
Christopher L. Harbo

Printed in the United States of America.
122016   010170R

TABLE OF CONTENTS

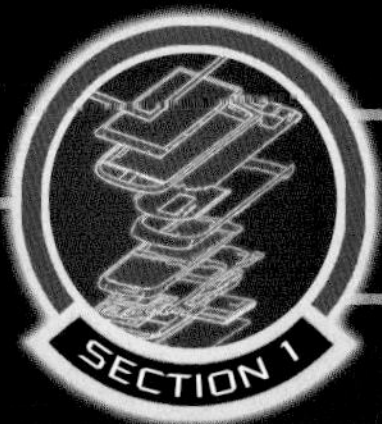
SECTION 1

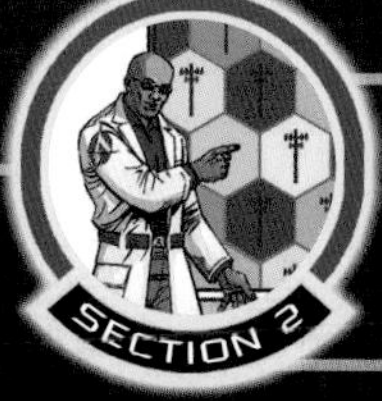
SECTION 2

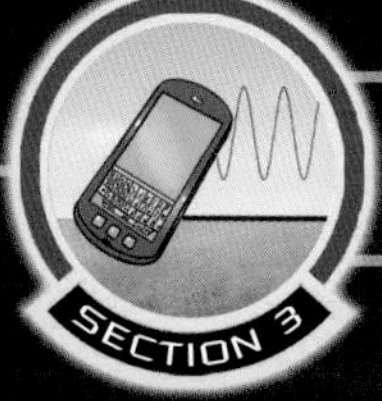
SECTION 3

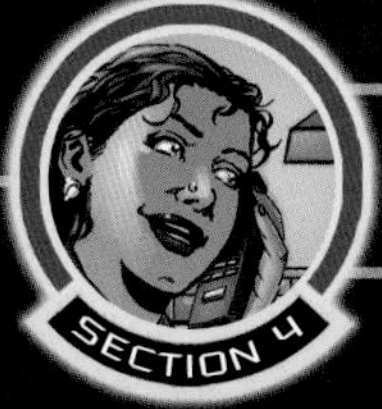
SECTION 4

SECTION 1 A DYNAMIC DEVICE

A visit to the Grand Canyon sparks an investigation into cell phone technology for Max Axiom, Super Scientist.

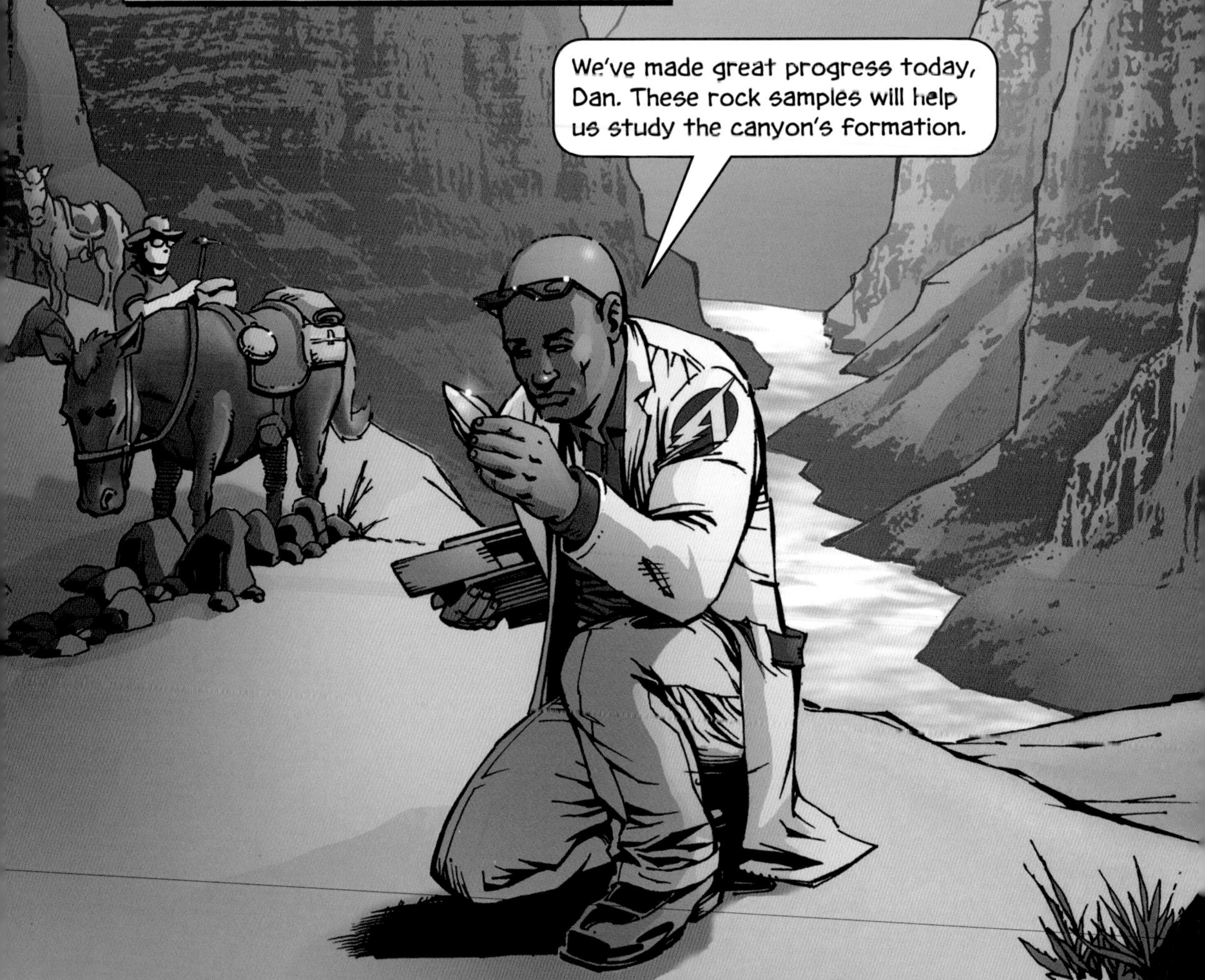
We've made great progress today, Dan. These rock samples will help us study the canyon's formation.

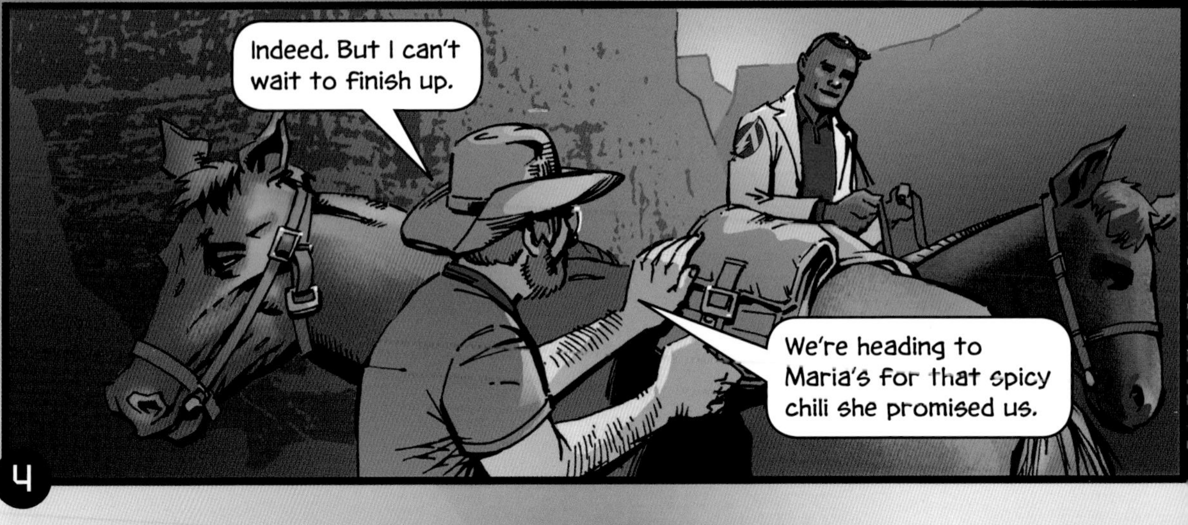
Indeed. But I can't wait to finish up.
We're heading to Maria's for that spicy chili she promised us.

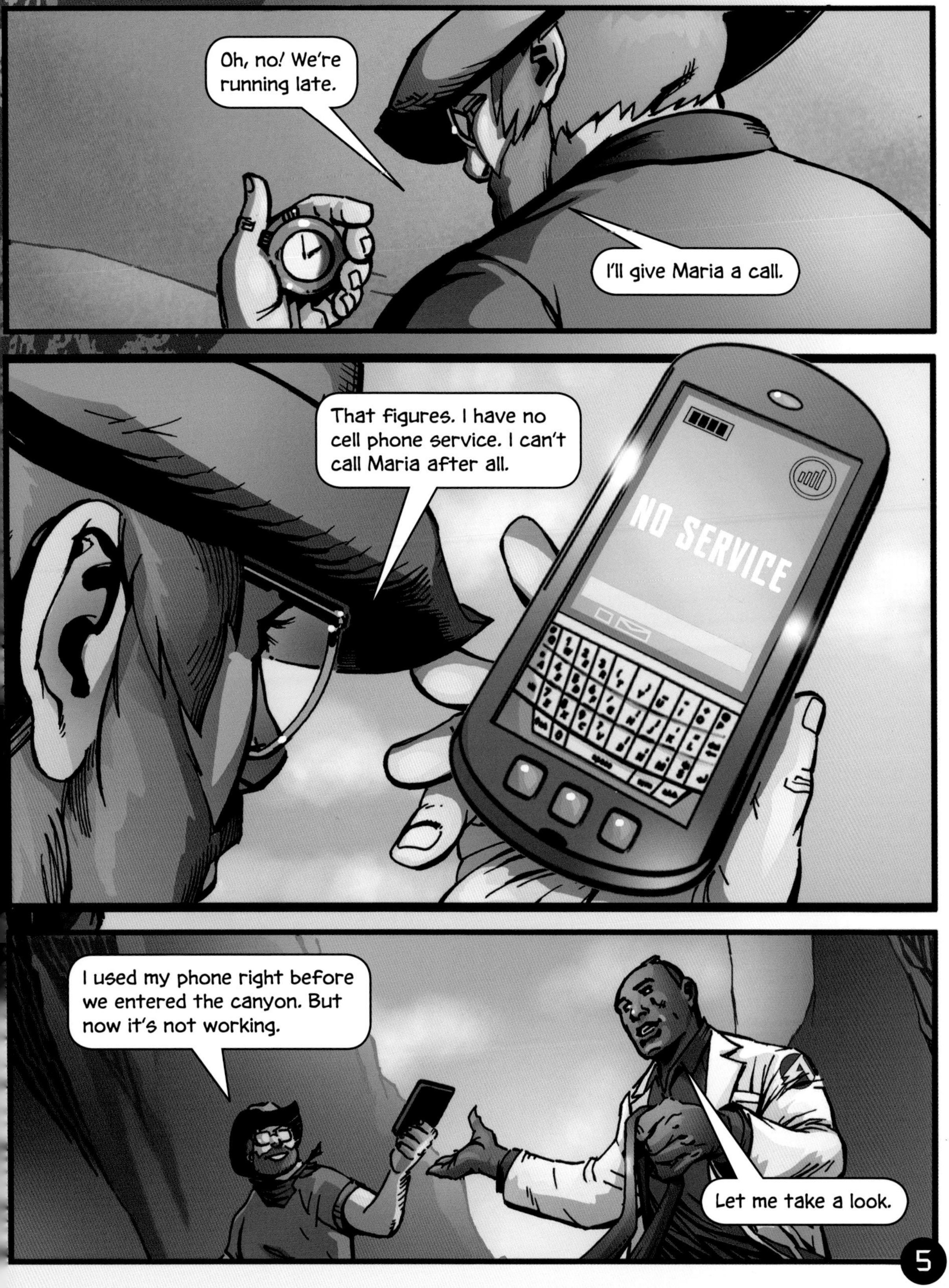
Oh, no! We're running late.
I'll give Maria a call.
That figures. I have no cell phone service. I can't call Maria after all.
NO SERVICE
I used my phone right before we entered the canyon. But now it's not working.
Let me take a look.

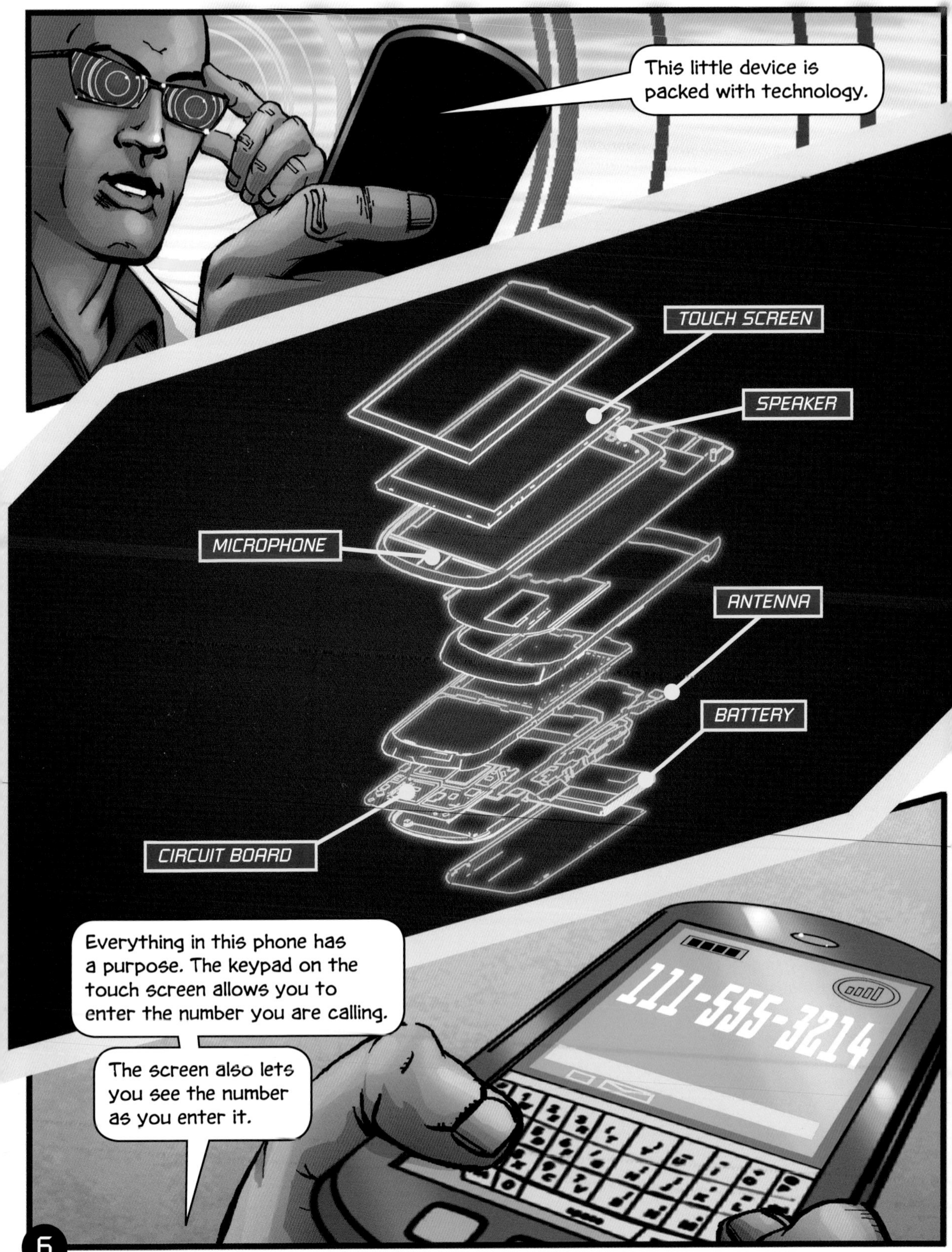

This little device is packed with technology.
TOUCH SCREEN
SPEAKER
MICROPHONE
ANTENNA
BATTERY
CIRCUIT BOARD
Everything in this phone has a purpose. The keypad on the touch screen allows you to enter the number you are calling.
The screen also lets you see the number as you enter it.
111-555-3214

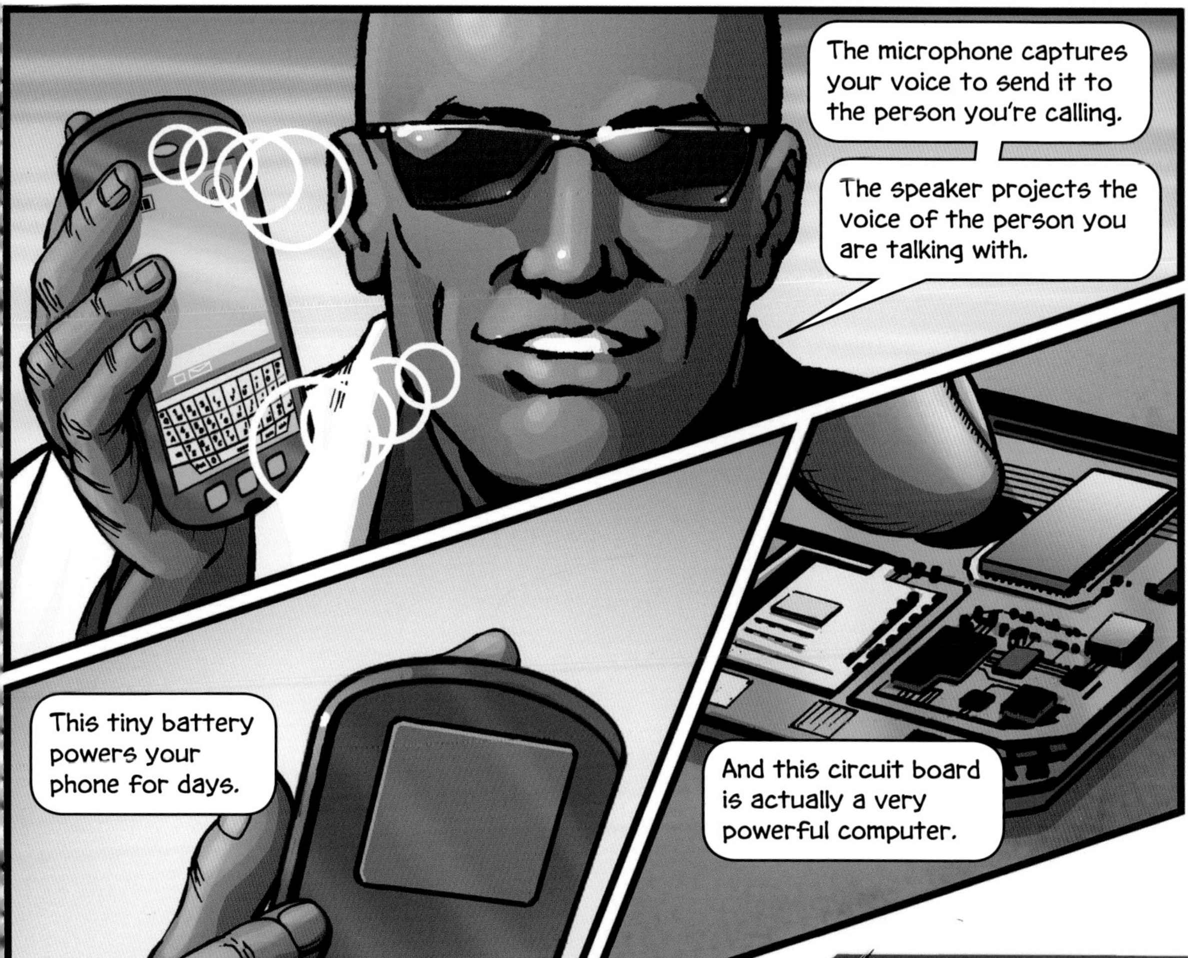

The microphone captures your voice to send it to the person you're calling.
The speaker projects the voice of the person you are talking with.
This tiny battery powers your phone for days.
And this circuit board is actually a very powerful computer.

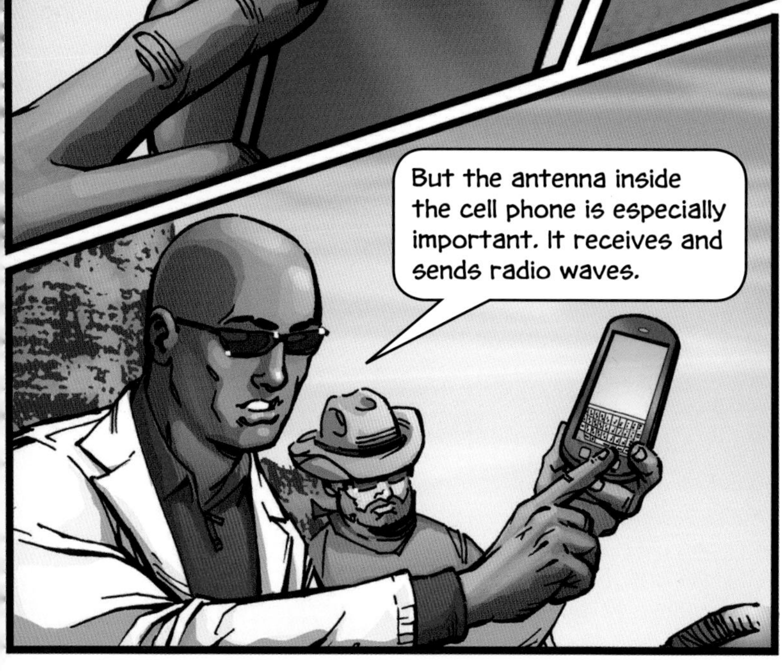

But the antenna inside the cell phone is especially important. It receives and sends radio waves.

BATTERIES

Cell phones need a long-lasting, small battery to be useful for everyday life. Lithium-ion battery technology provides the needed power. Without this technology, batteries would only last a short time, making cell phones impractical.

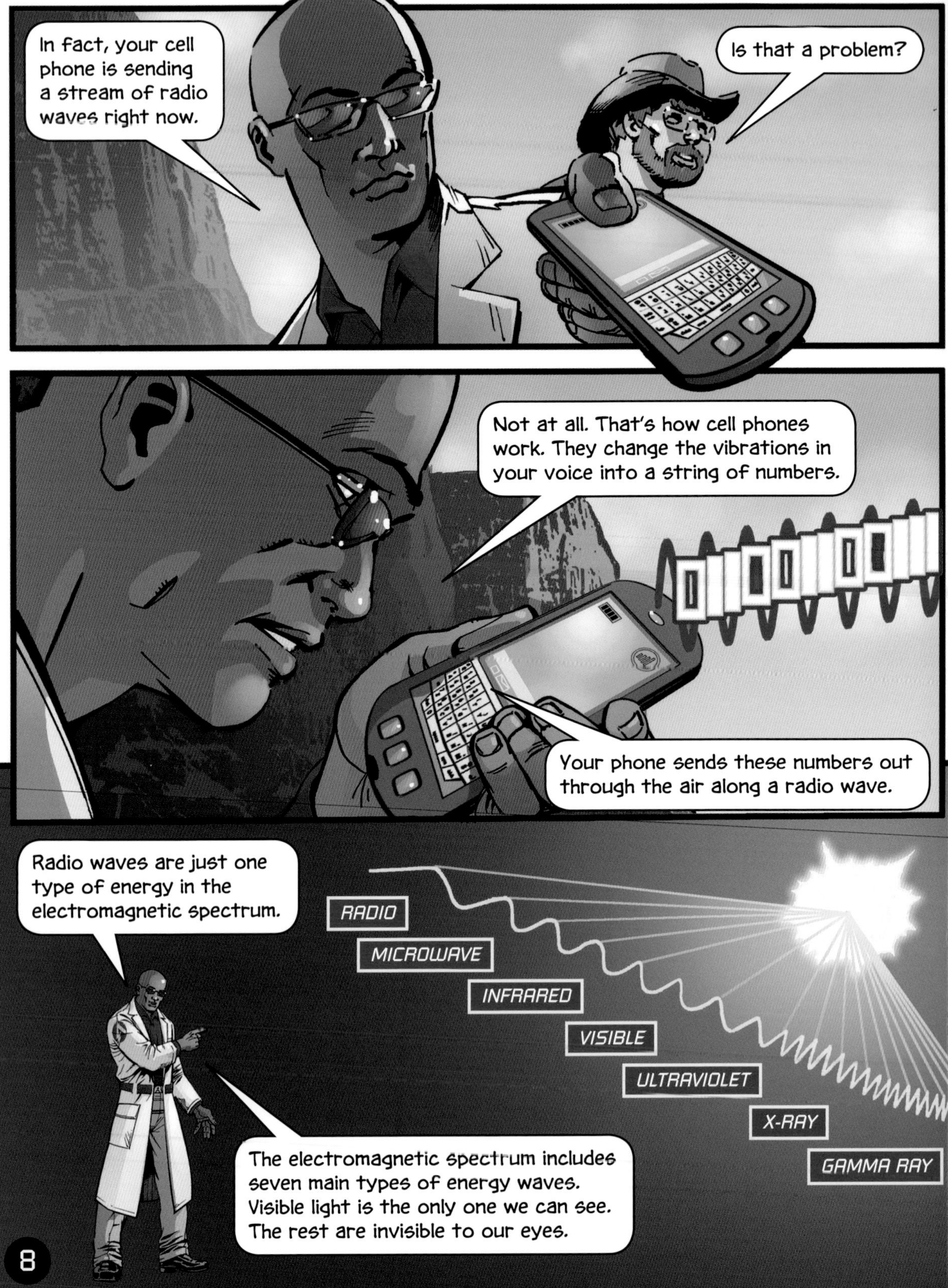
In fact, your cell phone is sending a stream of radio waves right now.
Is that a problem?
Not at all. That's how cell phones work. They change the vibrations in your voice into a string of numbers.
Your phone sends these numbers out through the air along a radio wave.
Radio waves are just one type of energy in the electromagnetic spectrum.
RADIO
MICROWAVE
INFRARED
VISIBLE
ULTRAVIOLET
X-RAY
GAMMA RAY
The electromagnetic spectrum includes seven main types of energy waves. Visible light is the only one we can see. The rest are invisible to our eyes.

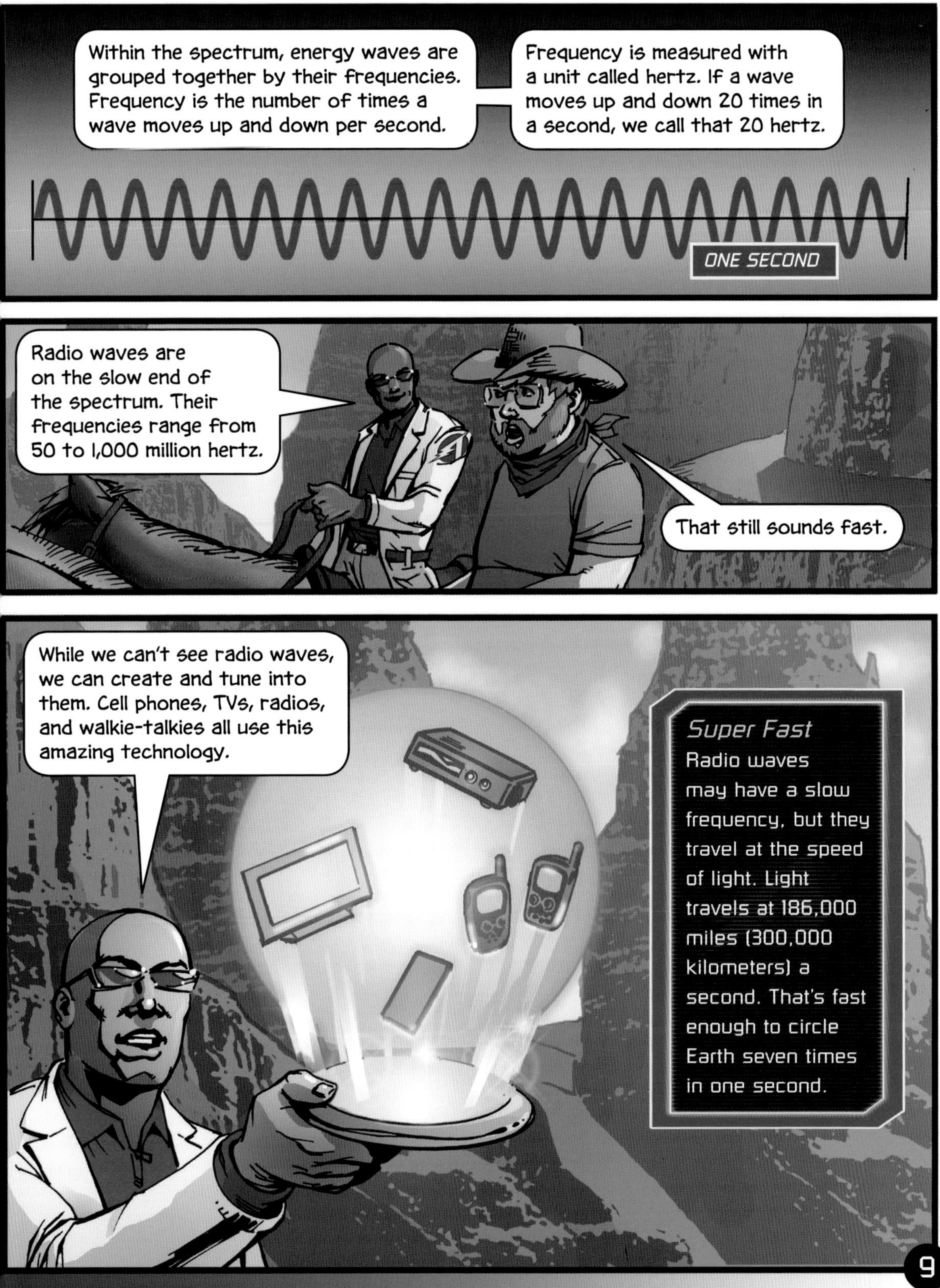
Within the spectrum, energy waves are grouped together by their frequencies. Frequency is the number of times a wave moves up and down per second.
Frequency is measured with a unit called hertz. If a wave moves up and down 20 times in a second, we call that 20 hertz.
ONE SECOND
Radio waves are on the slow end of the spectrum. Their frequencies range from 50 to 1,000 million hertz.
That still sounds fast.
While we can't see radio waves, we can create and tune into them. Cell phones, TVs, radios, and walkie-talkies all use this amazing technology.
Super Fast
Radio waves may have a slow frequency, but they travel at the speed of light. Light travels at 186,000 miles (300,000 kilometers) a second. That's fast enough to circle Earth seven times in one second.

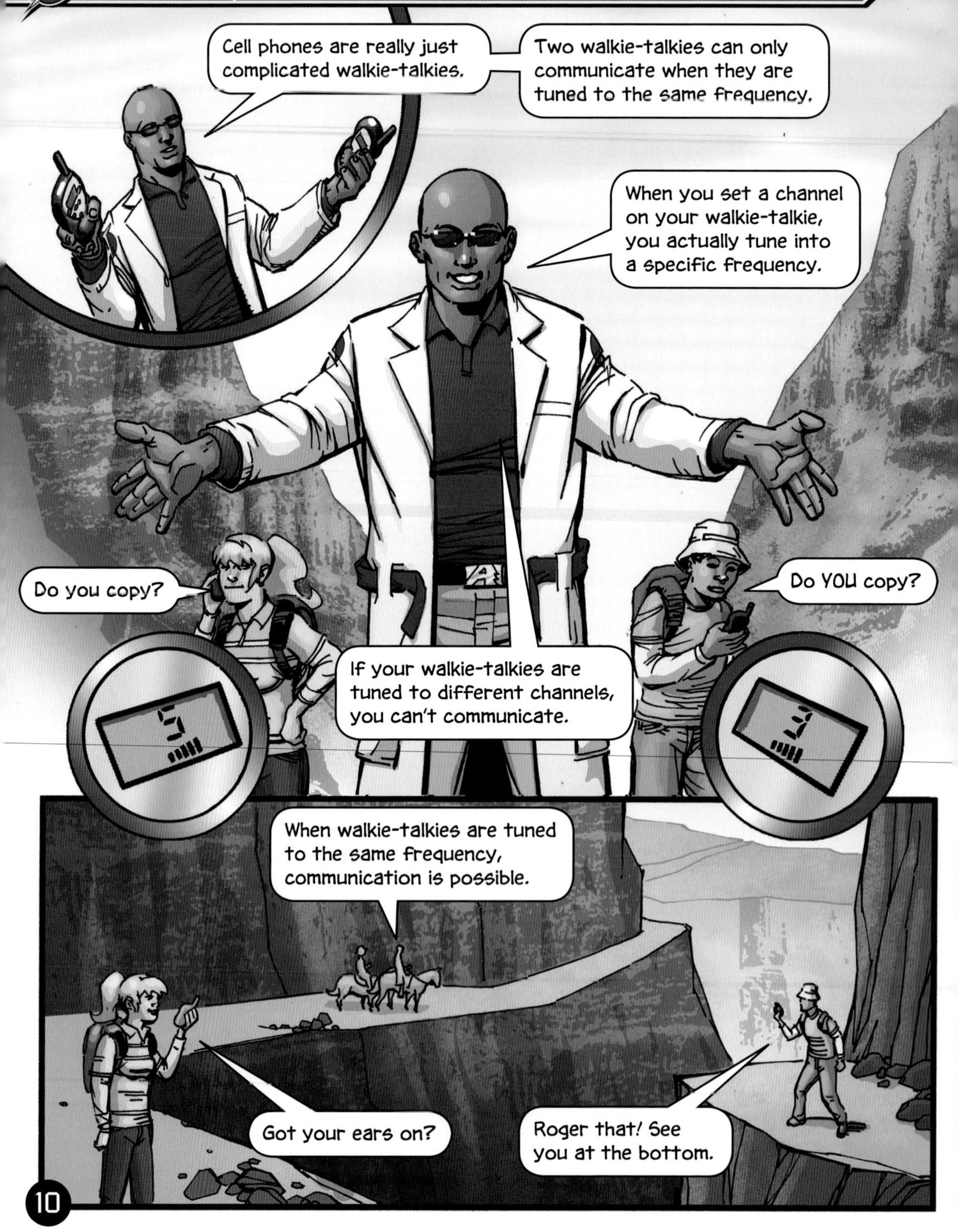
Cell phones are really just complicated walkie-talkies.
Two walkie-talkies can only communicate when they are tuned to the same frequency.
When you set a channel on your walkie-talkie, you actually tune into a specific frequency.
Do you copy?
Do YOU copy?
If your walkie-talkies are tuned to different channels, you can't communicate.
5
3
When walkie-talkies are tuned to the same frequency, communication is possible.
Got your ears on?
Roger that! See you at the bottom.

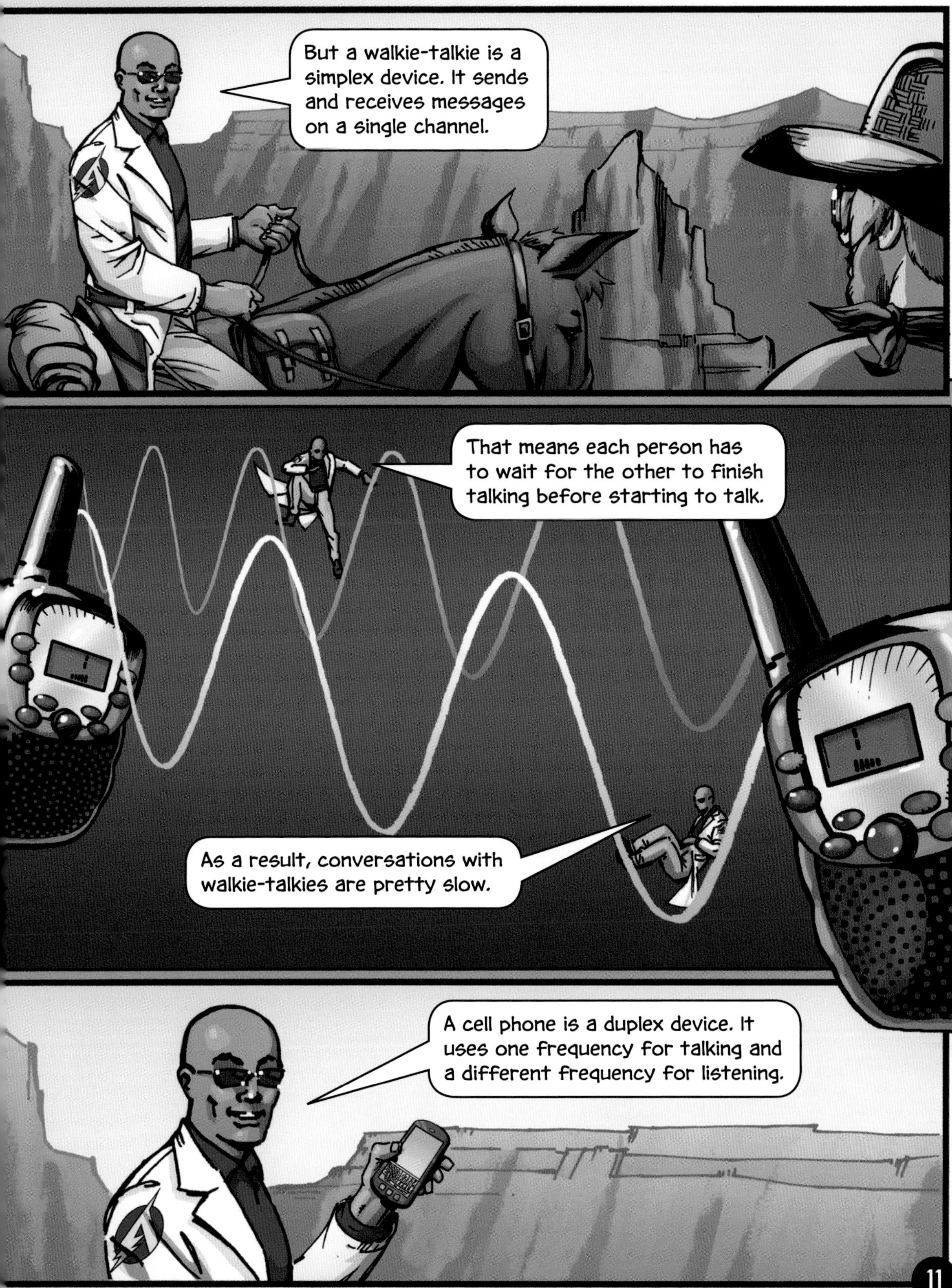
But a walkie-talkie is a simplex device. It sends and receives messages on a single channel.
That means each person has to wait for the other to finish talking before starting to talk.
As a result, conversations with walkie-talkies are pretty slow.
A cell phone is a duplex device. It uses one frequency for talking and a different frequency for listening.

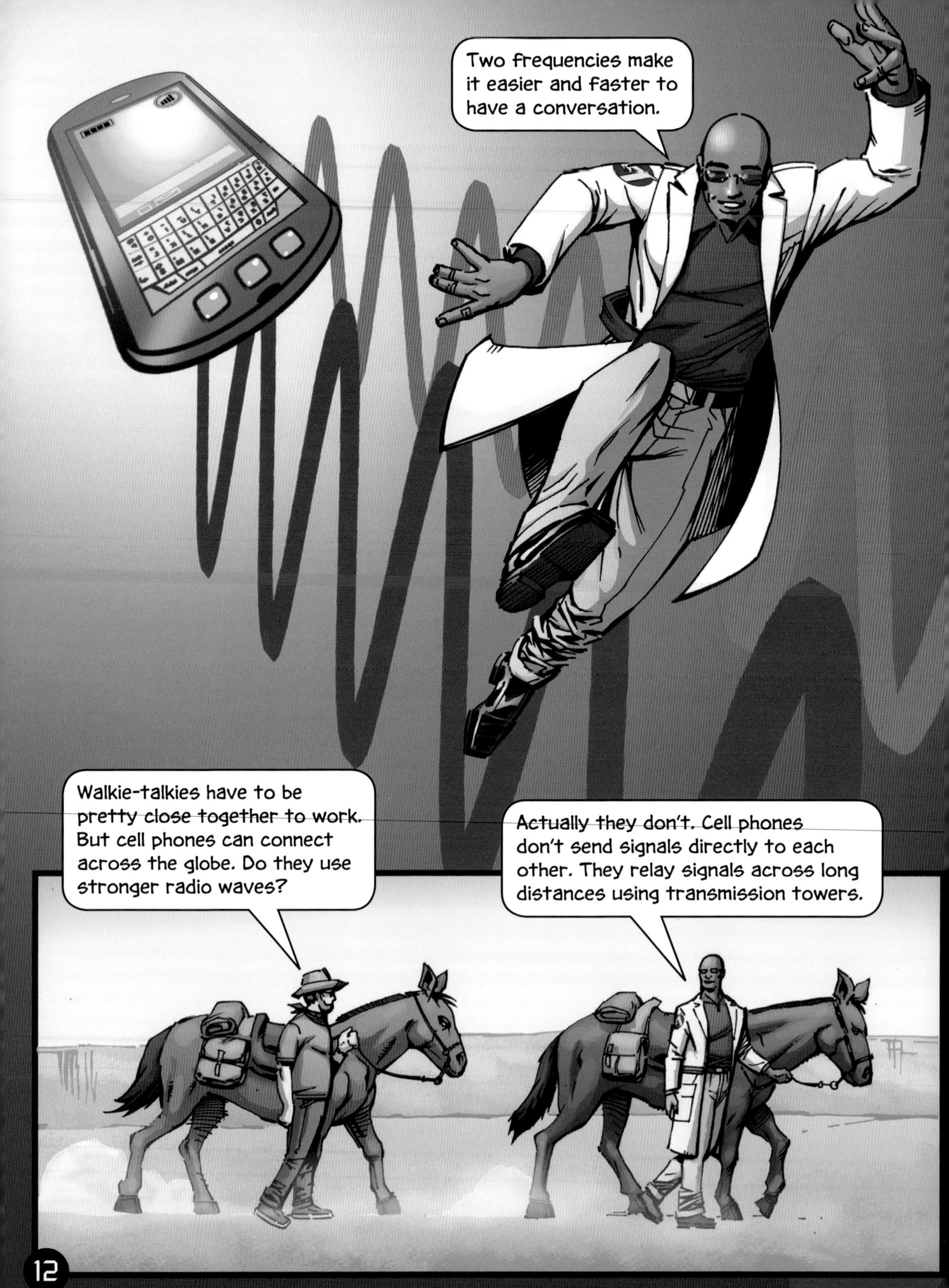
Two frequencies make it easier and faster to have a conversation.
Walkie-talkies have to be pretty close together to work. But cell phones can connect across the globe. Do they use stronger radio waves?
Actually they don't. Cell phones don't send signals directly to each other. They relay signals across long distances using transmission towers.

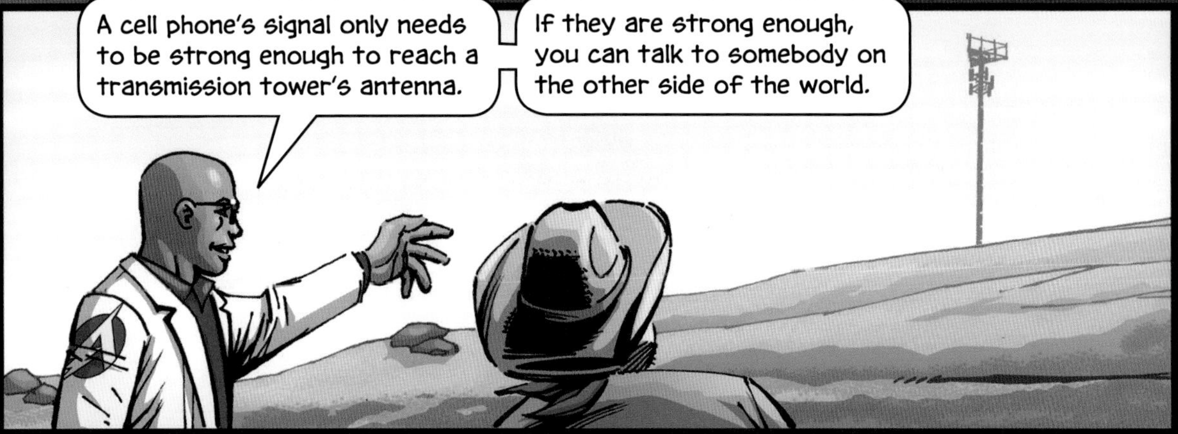
A cell phone's signal only needs to be strong enough to reach a transmission tower's antenna.
If they are strong enough, you can talk to somebody on the other side of the world.

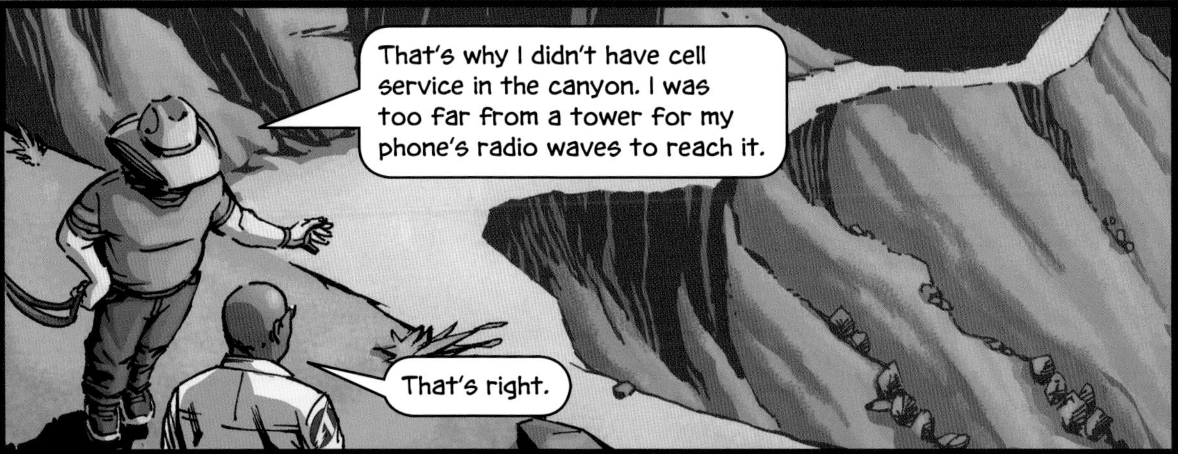
That's why I didn't have cell service in the canyon. I was too far from a tower for my phone's radio waves to reach it.
That's right.

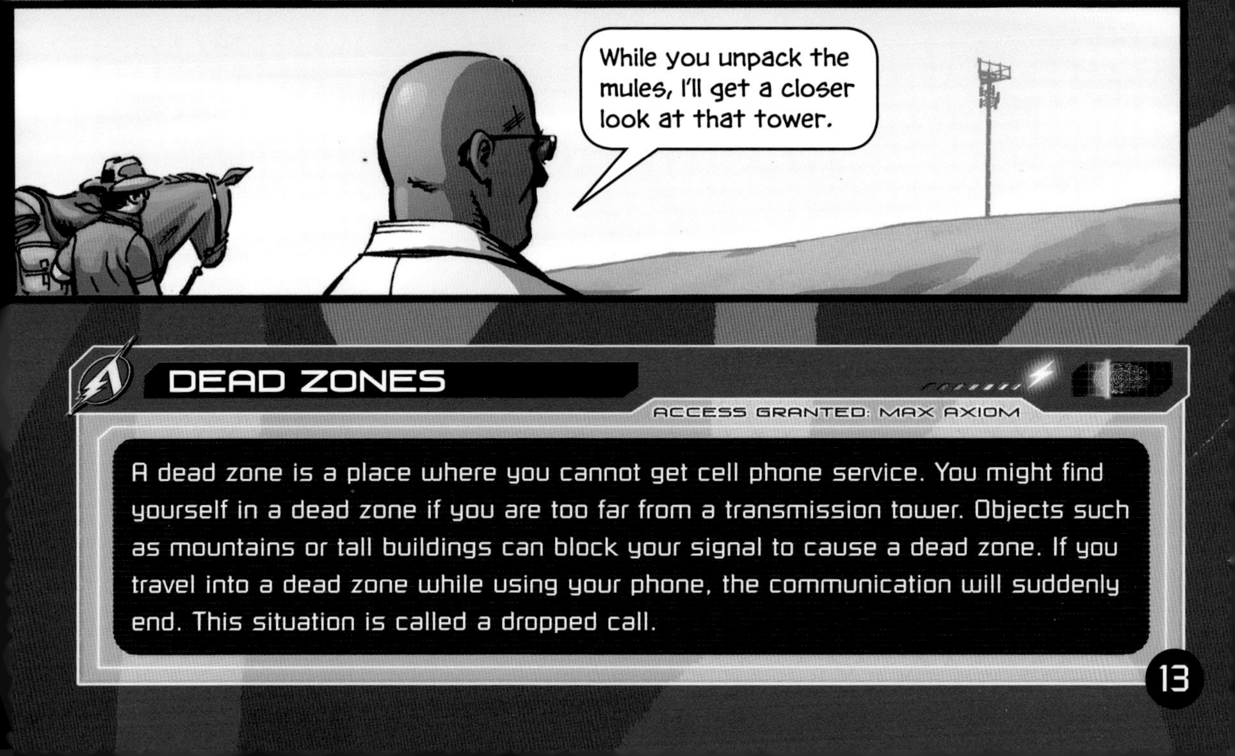
While you unpack the mules, I'll get a closer look at that tower.

DEAD ZONES

ACCESS GRANTED: MAX AXIOM

A dead zone is a place where you cannot get cell phone service. You might find yourself in a dead zone if you are too far from a transmission tower. Objects such as mountains or tall buildings can block your signal to cause a dead zone. If you travel into a dead zone while using your phone, the communication will suddenly end. This situation is called a dropped call.

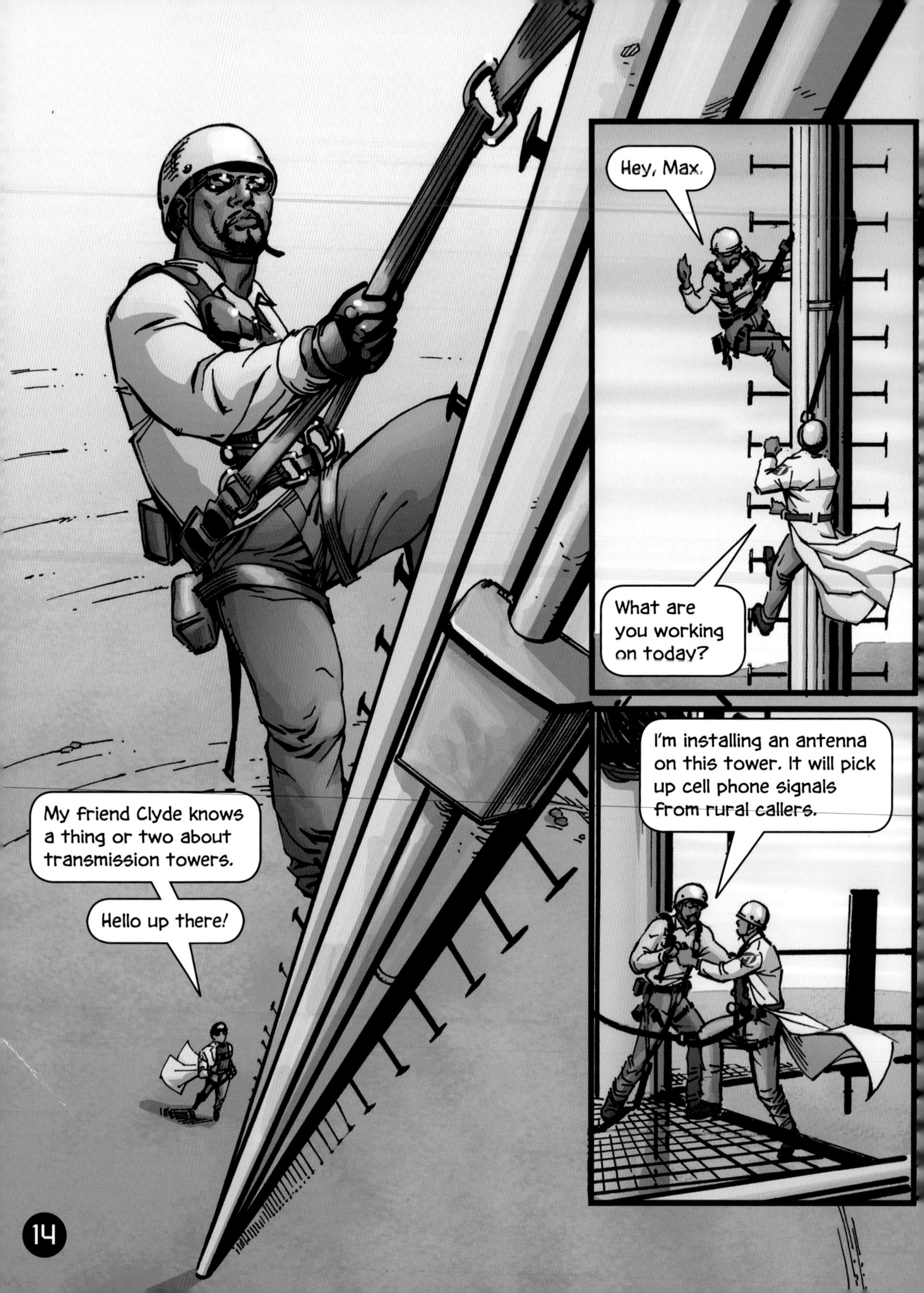

My friend Clyde knows a thing or two about transmission towers.
Hello up there!
Hey, Max.
What are you working on today?
I'm installing an antenna on this tower. It will pick up cell phone signals from rural callers.

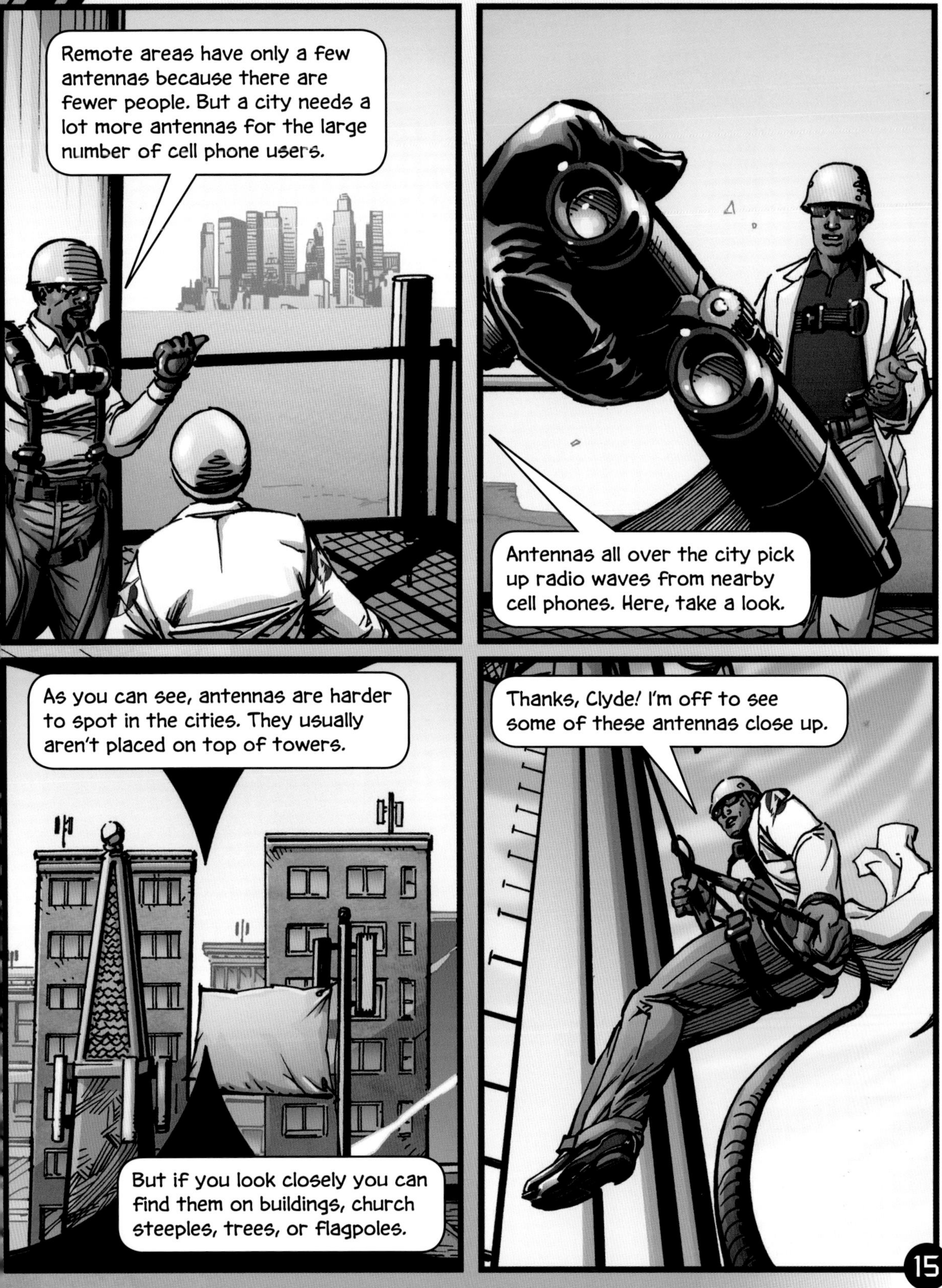
Remote areas have only a few antennas because there are fewer people. But a city needs a lot more antennas for the large number of cell phone users.
Antennas all over the city pick up radio waves from nearby cell phones. Here, take a look.
As you can see, antennas are harder to spot in the cities. They usually aren't placed on top of towers.
But if you look closely you can find them on buildings, church steeples, trees, or flagpoles.
Thanks, Clyde! I'm off to see some of these antennas close up.

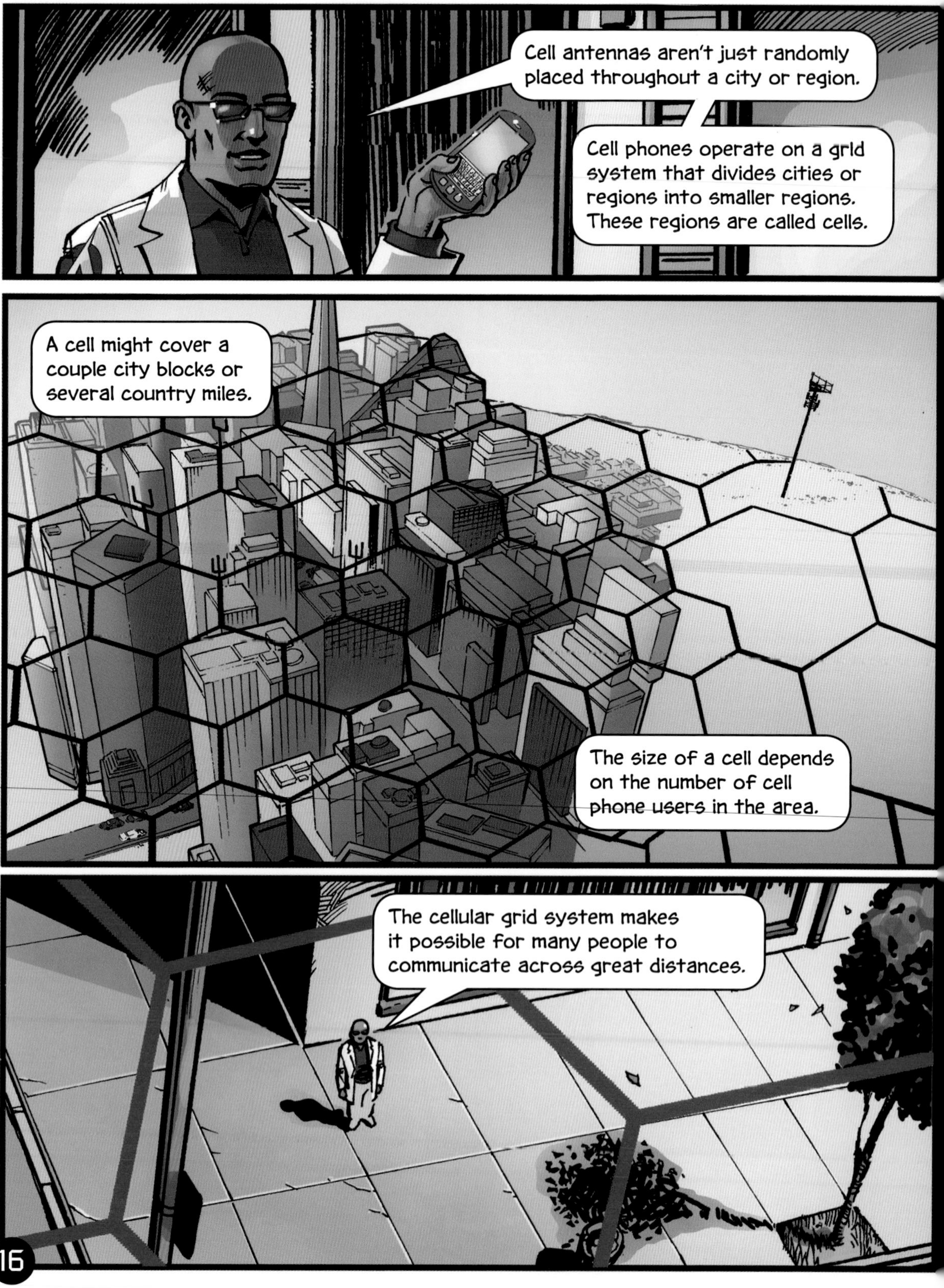
Cell antennas aren't just randomly placed throughout a city or region.
Cell phones operate on a grid system that divides cities or regions into smaller regions. These regions are called cells.
A cell might cover a couple city blocks or several country miles.
The size of a cell depends on the number of cell phone users in the area.
The cellular grid system makes it possible for many people to communicate across great distances.

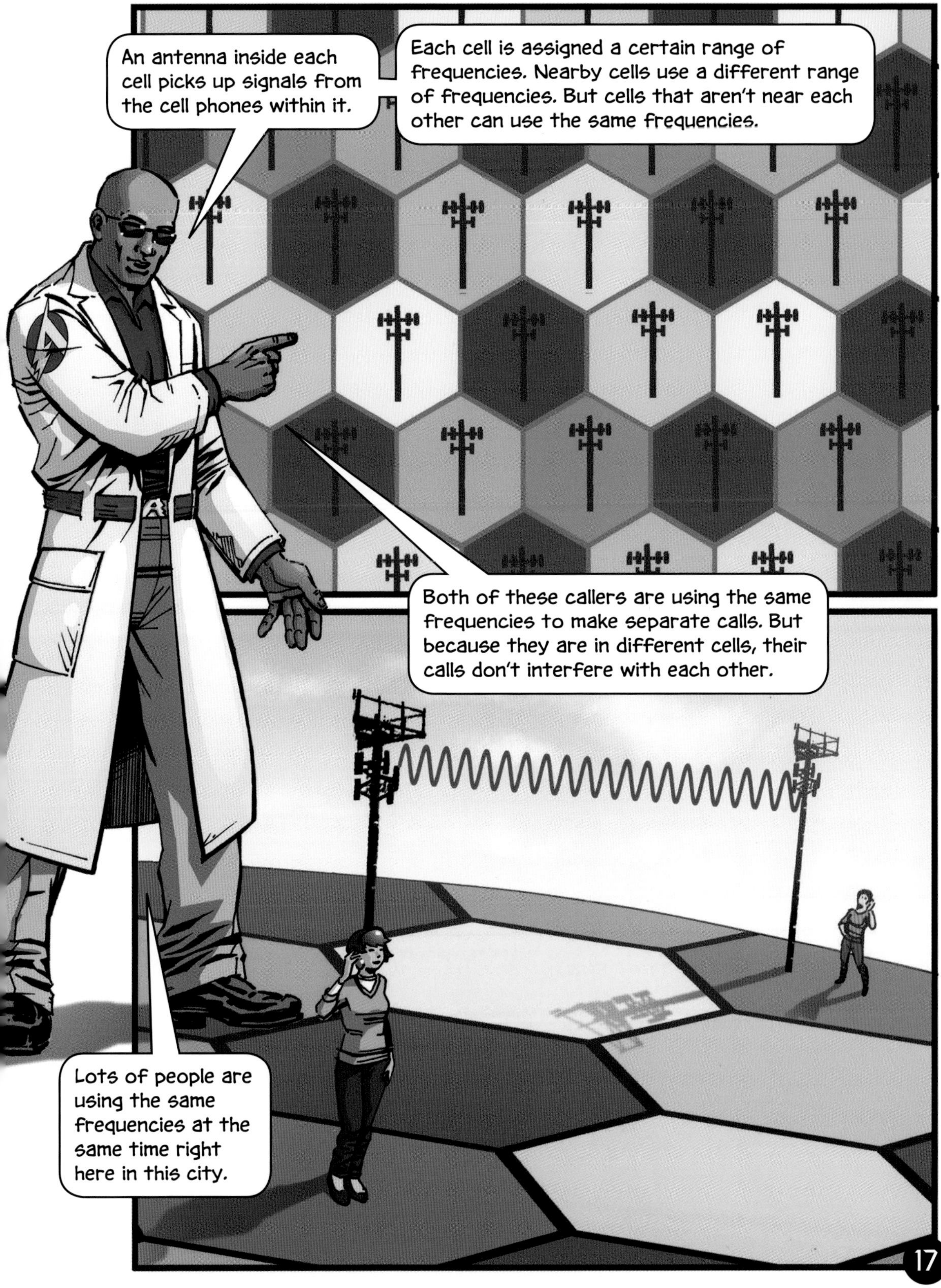

An antenna inside each cell picks up signals from the cell phones within it.
Each cell is assigned a certain range of frequencies. Nearby cells use a different range of frequencies. But cells that aren't near each other can use the same frequencies.
Both of these callers are using the same frequencies to make separate calls. But because they are in different cells, their calls don't interfere with each other.
Lots of people are using the same frequencies at the same time right here in this city.

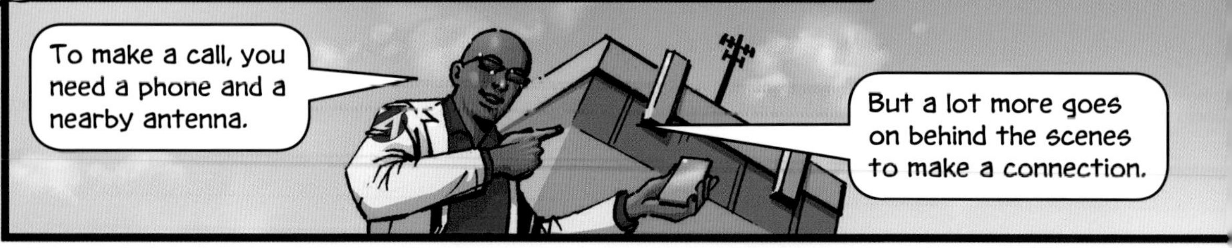
To make a call, you need a phone and a nearby antenna.
But a lot more goes on behind the scenes to make a connection.

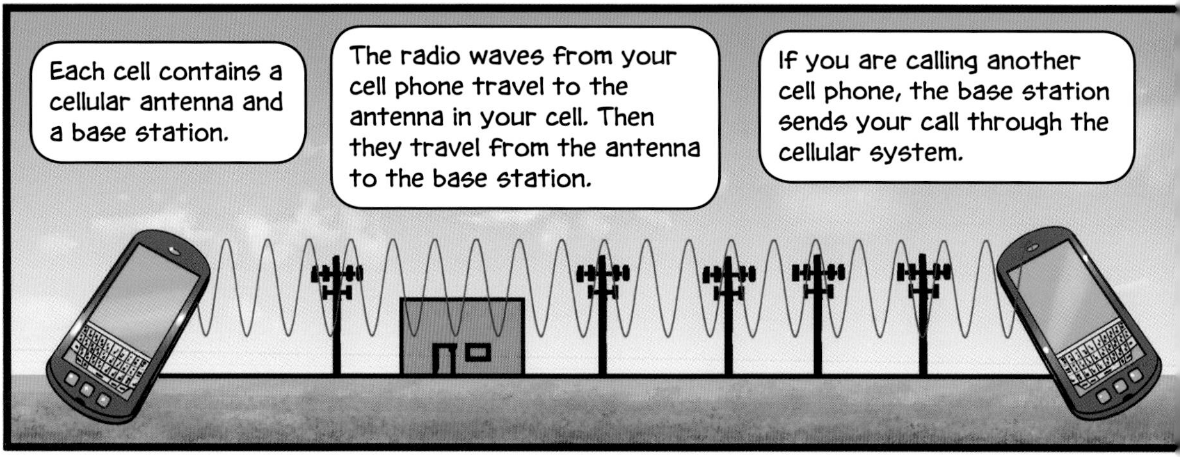
Each cell contains a cellular antenna and a base station.
The radio waves from your cell phone travel to the antenna in your cell. Then they travel from the antenna to the base station.
If you are calling another cell phone, the base station sends your call through the cellular system.

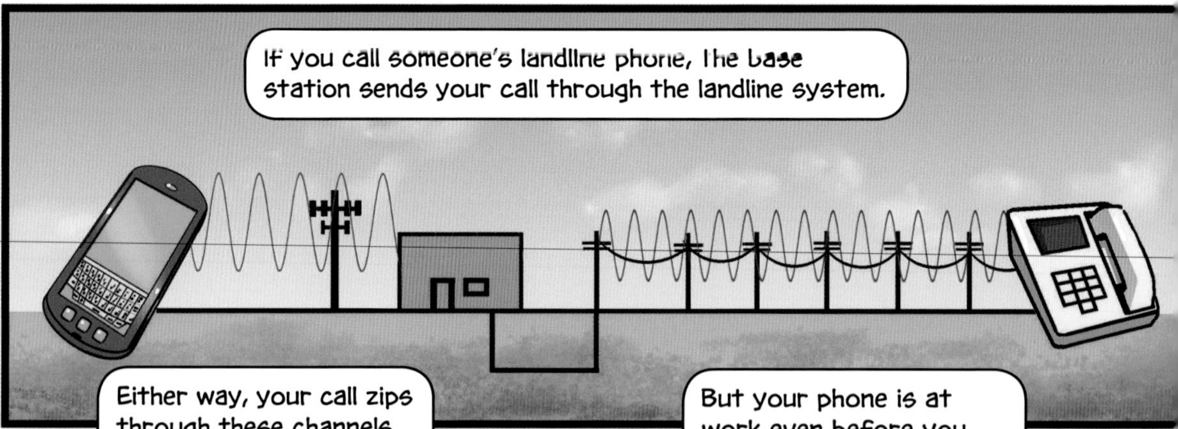
If you call someone's landline phone, the base station sends your call through the landline system.

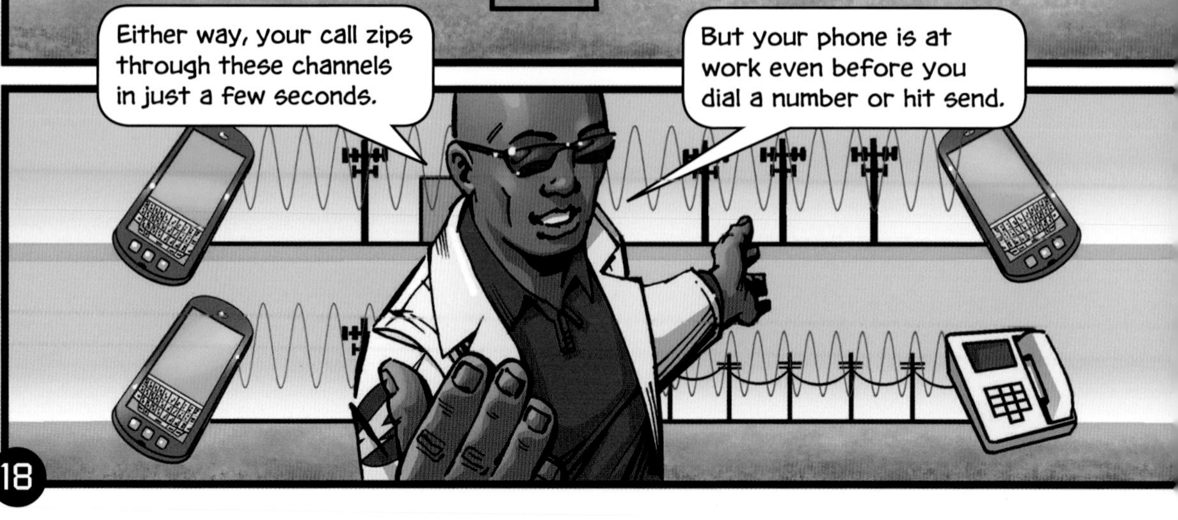
Either way, your call zips through these channels in just a few seconds.
But your phone is at work even before you dial a number or hit send.

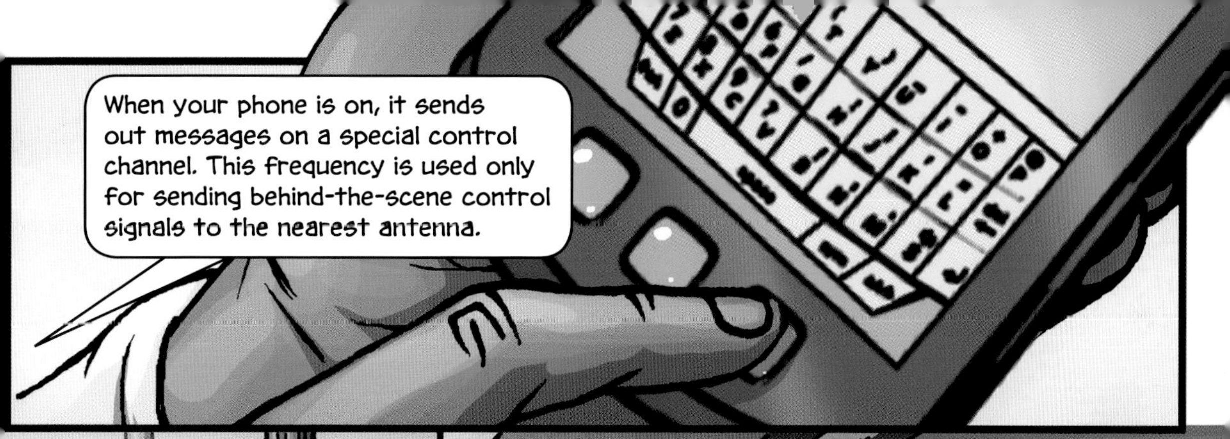
When your phone is on, it sends out messages on a special control channel. This frequency is used only for sending behind-the-scene control signals to the nearest antenna.

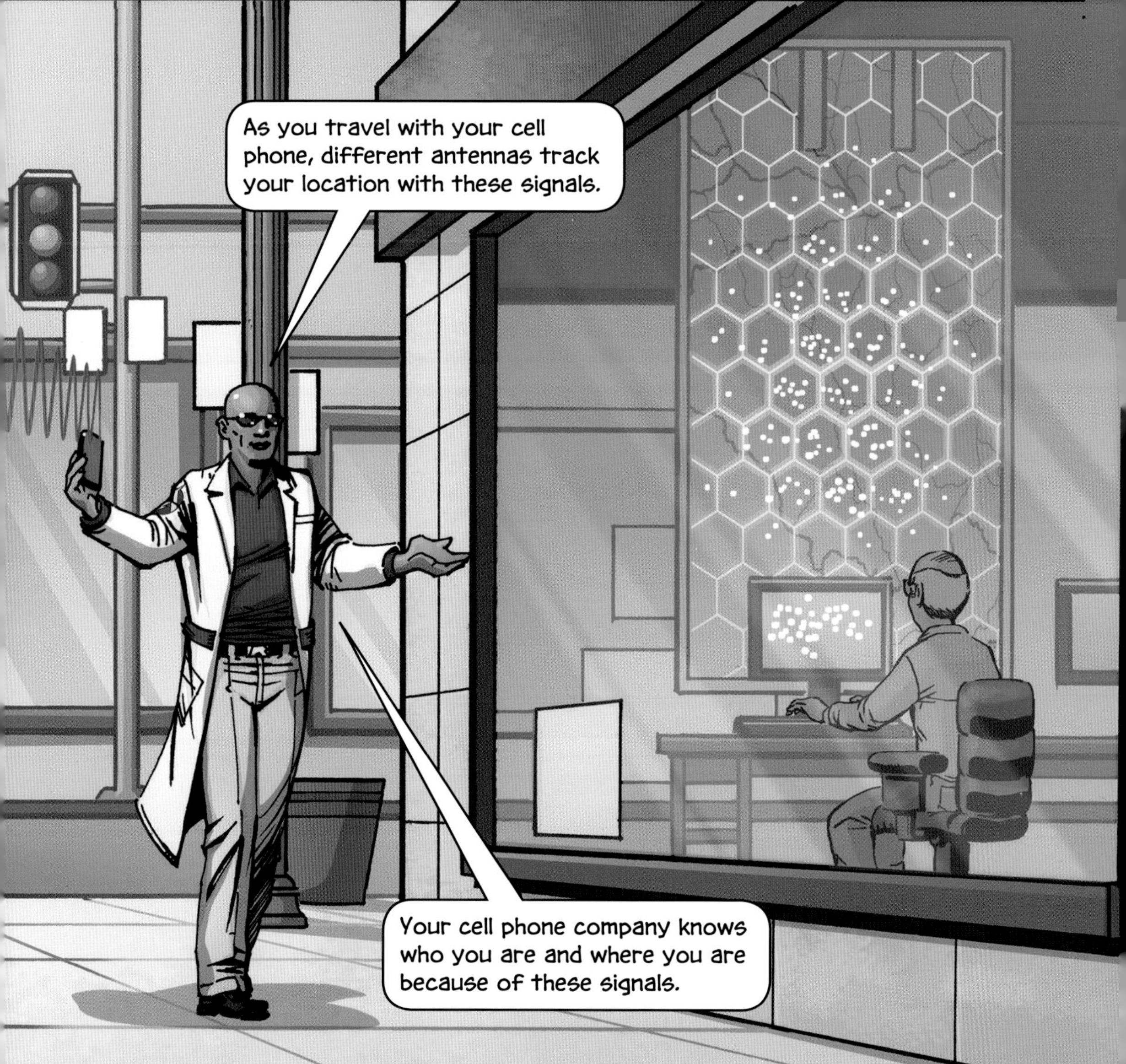
As you travel with your cell phone, different antennas track your location with these signals.
Your cell phone company knows who you are and where you are because of these signals.

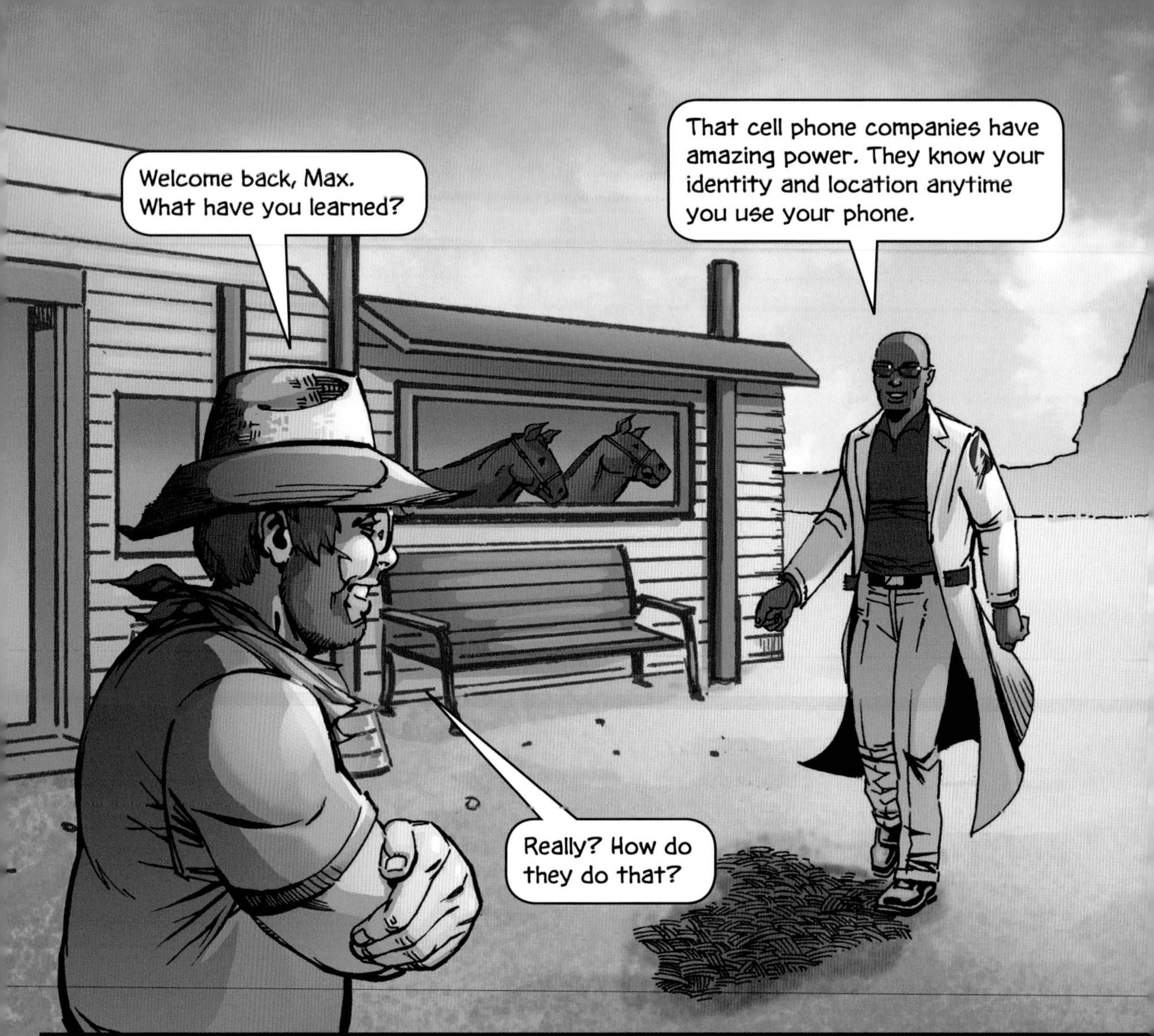
Welcome back, Max. What have you learned?
That cell phone companies have amazing power. They know your identity and location anytime you use your phone.
Really? How do they do that?

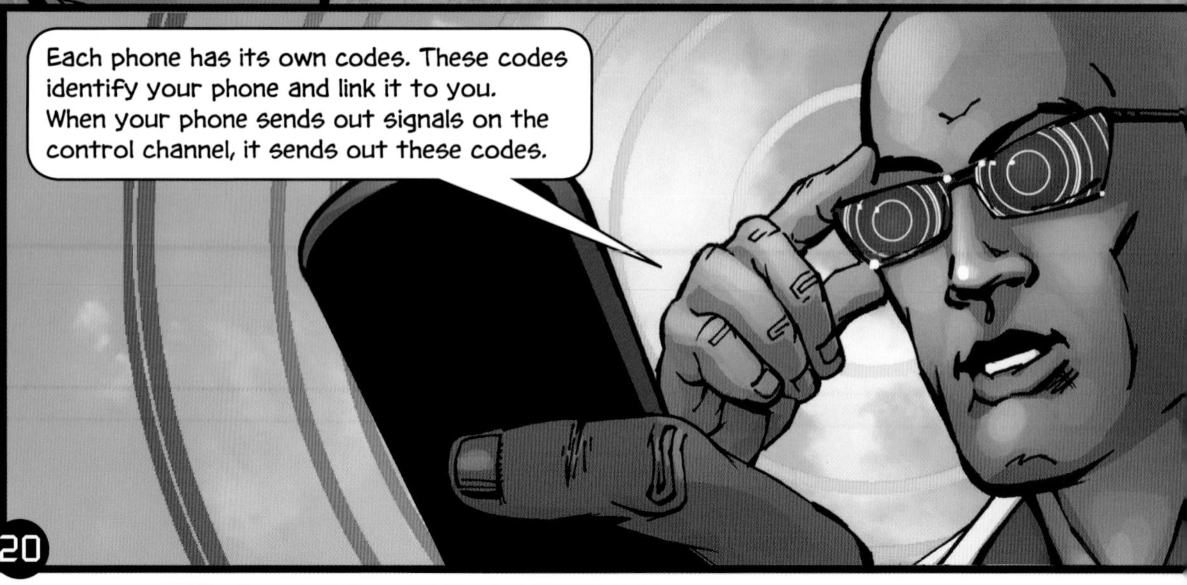
Each phone has its own codes. These codes identify your phone and link it to you. When your phone sends out signals on the control channel, it sends out these codes.

The electronic serial number (ESN) identifies your phone.

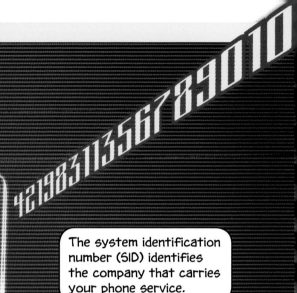

The mobile identification number (MIN) is your phone number.

The system identification number (SID) identifies the company that carries your phone service.

Your phone sends out these three numbers as it goes from cell to cell. They tell your phone company where you are and how many minutes you talk on your phone each month.

BILL
MINUTES USED

The control channel signals allow you to make calls. They also help locate you when someone is trying to call you.

ROAMING

Even if you travel in areas where your cell phone company doesn't operate, other companies will carry your phone calls. But they usually charge you extra money to do it. This charge is for what phone companies call "roaming."

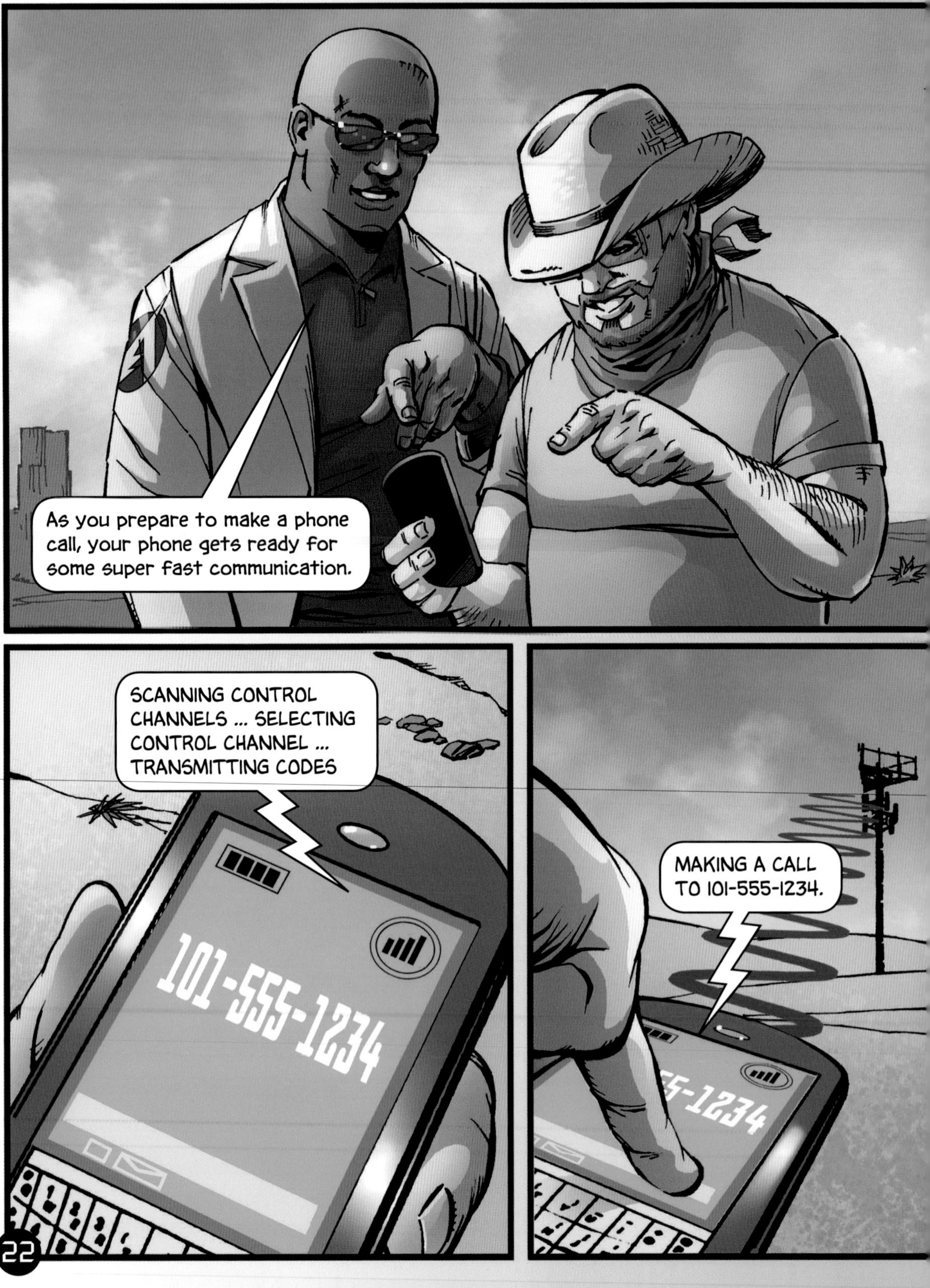
As you prepare to make a phone call, your phone gets ready for some super fast communication.
SCANNING CONTROL CHANNELS ... SELECTING CONTROL CHANNEL ... TRANSMITTING CODES
101-555-1234
MAKING A CALL TO 101-555-1234.
5-1234

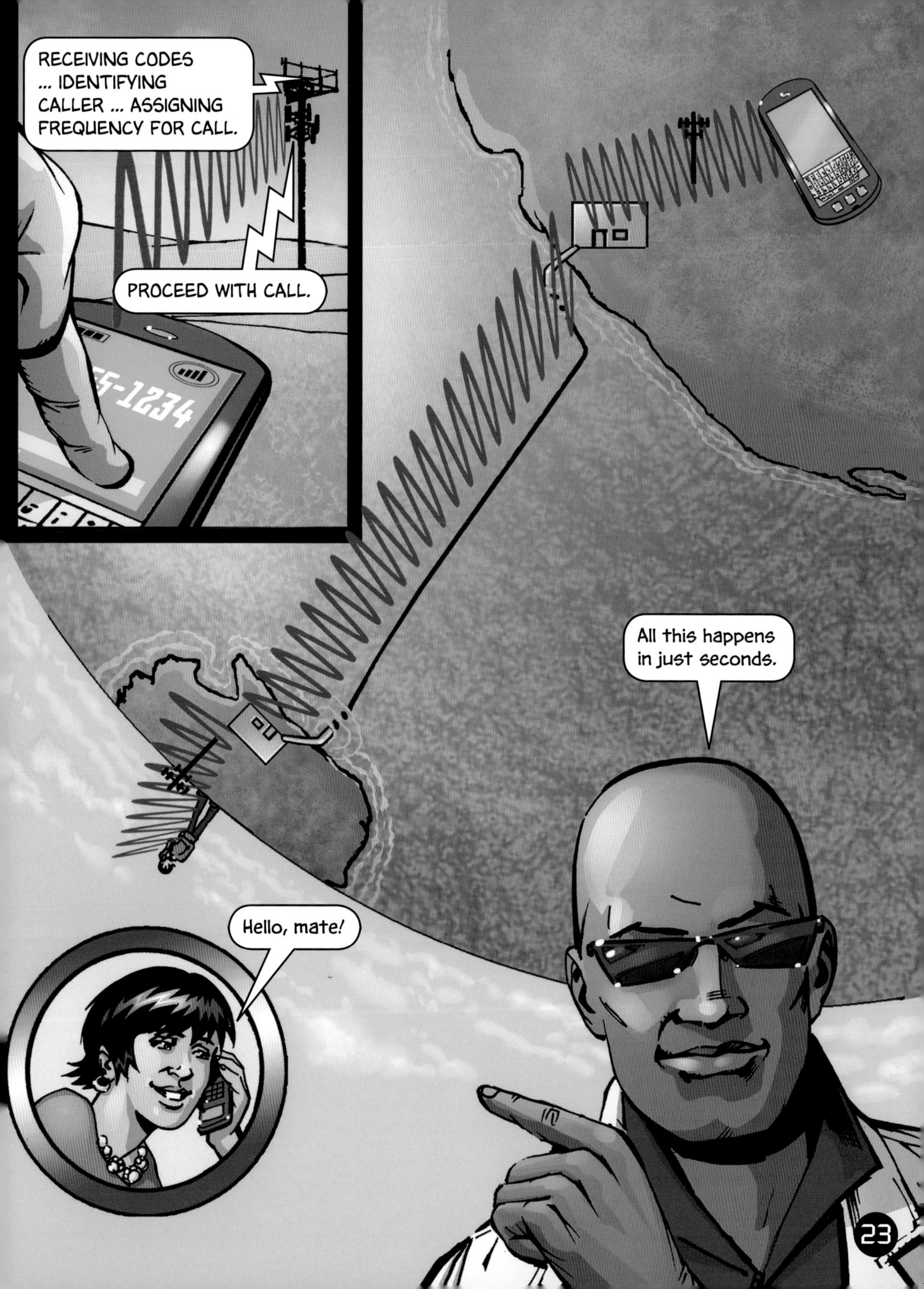
RECEIVING CODES ... IDENTIFYING CALLER ... ASSIGNING FREQUENCY FOR CALL.
PROCEED WITH CALL.
55-1234
All this happens in just seconds.
Hello, mate!

SECTION 4 | MAKING THE CALL

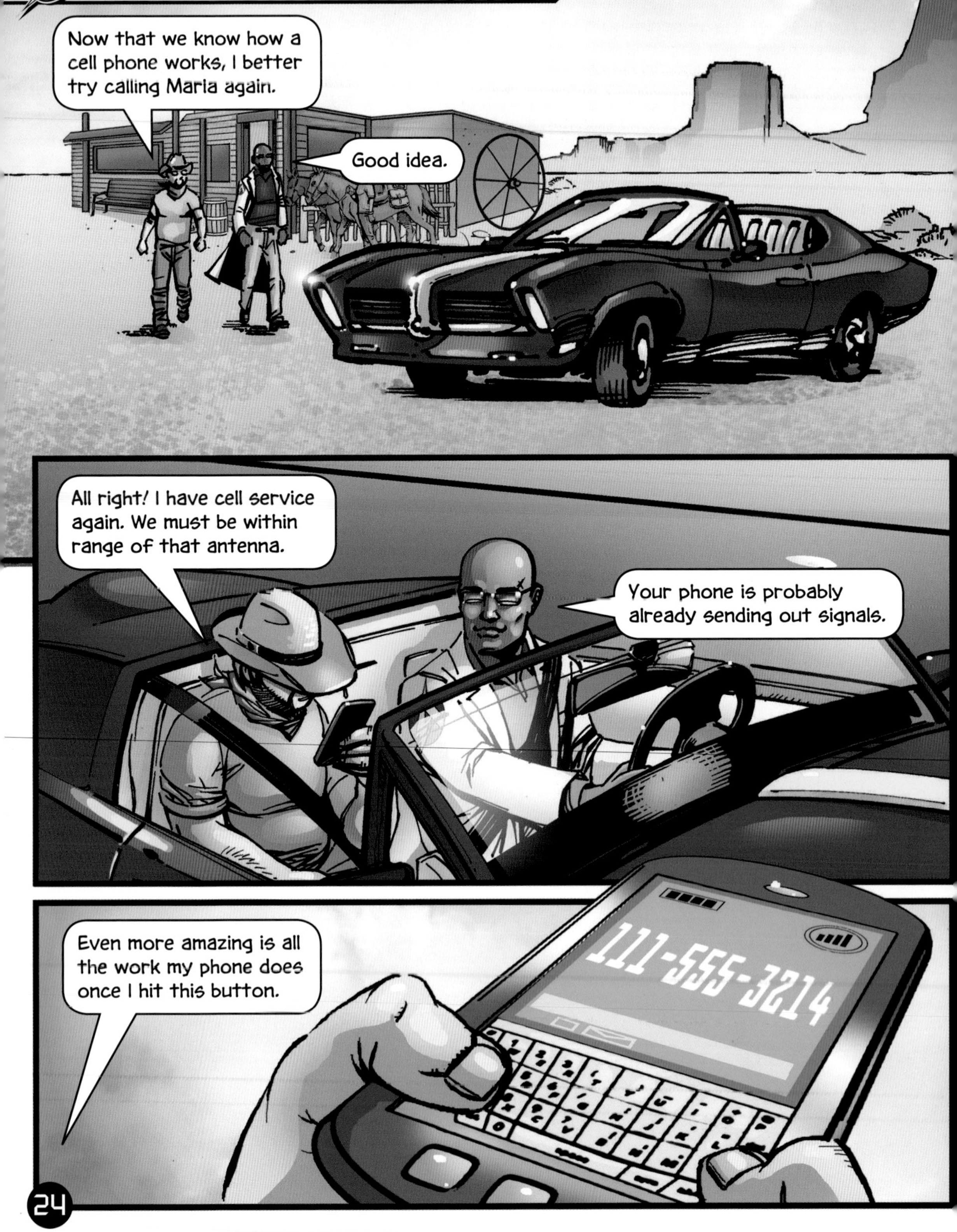

Now that we know how a cell phone works, I better try calling Maria again.
Good idea.
All right! I have cell service again. We must be within range of that antenna.
Your phone is probably already sending out signals.
Even more amazing is all the work my phone does once I hit this button.
111-555-3214

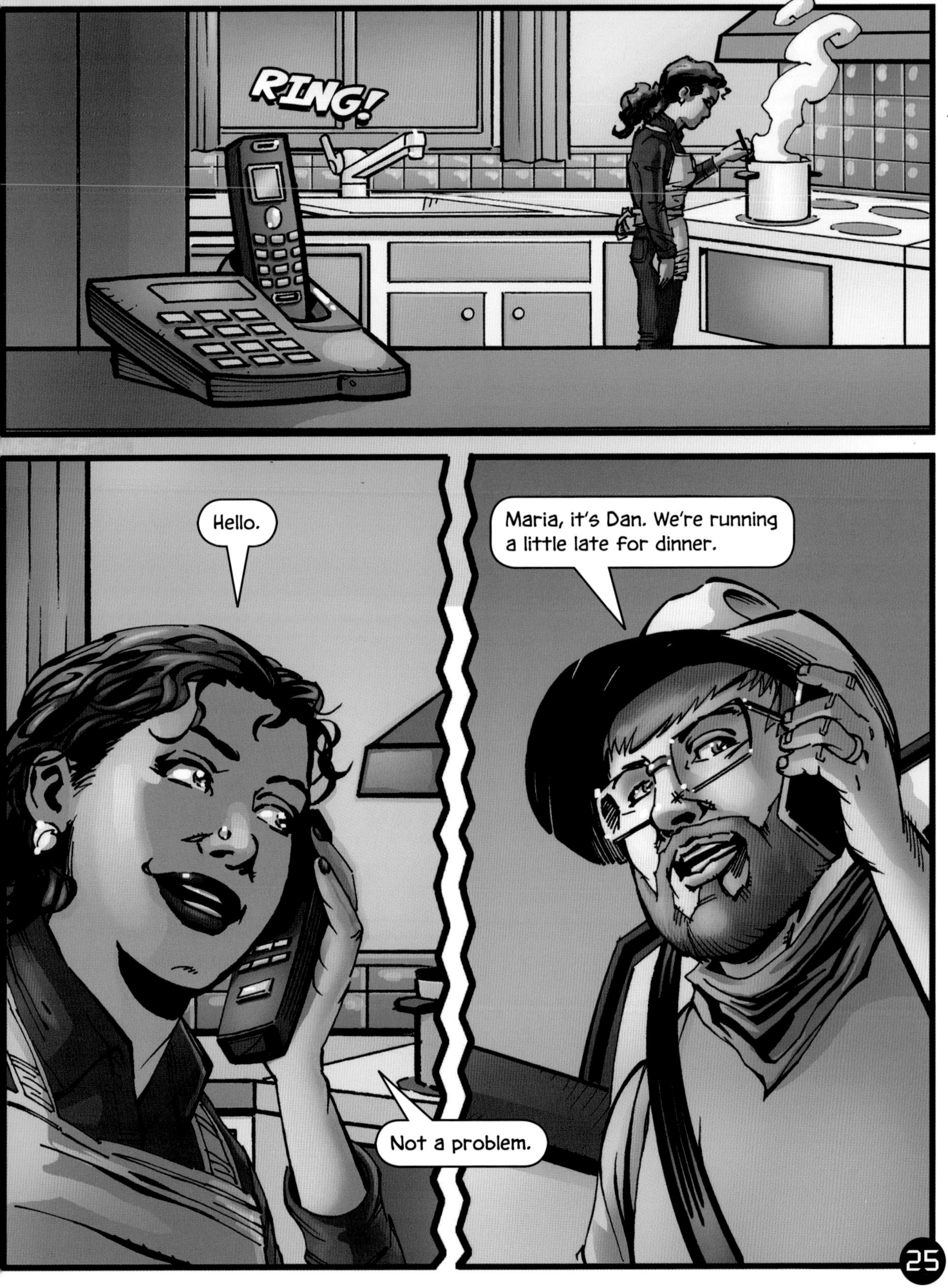
RING!
Hello.
Maria, it's Dan. We're running a little late for dinner.
Not a problem.

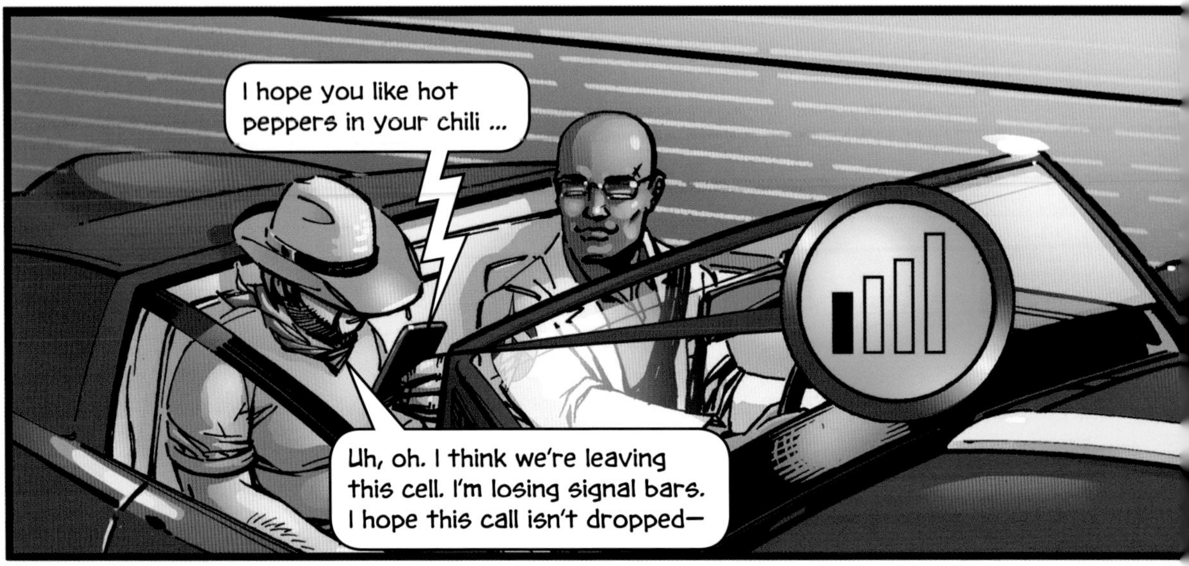
I hope you like hot peppers in your chili ...
Uh, oh. I think we're leaving this cell. I'm losing signal bars. I hope this call isn't dropped—

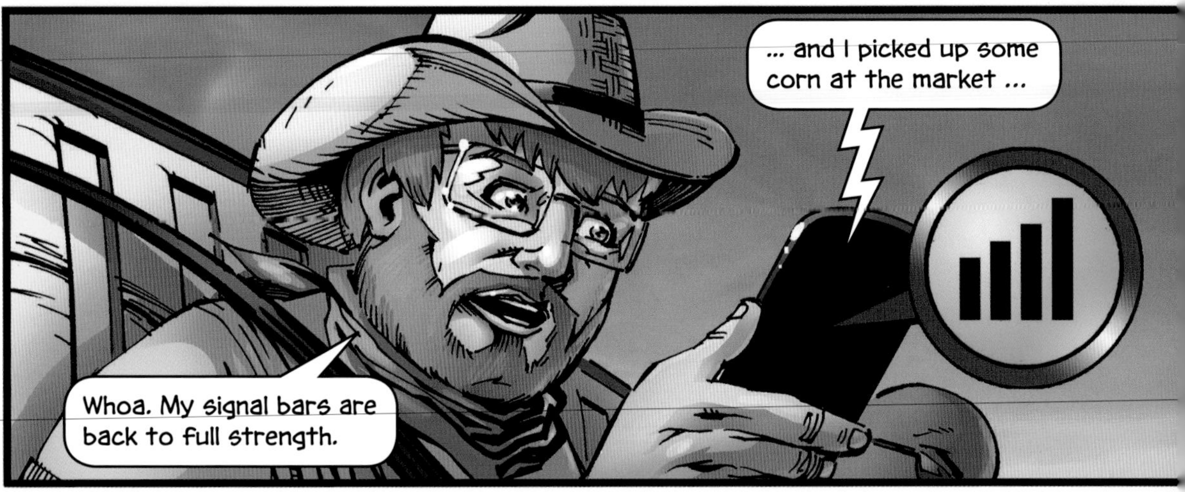
... and I picked up some corn at the market ...
Whoa. My signal bars are back to full strength.

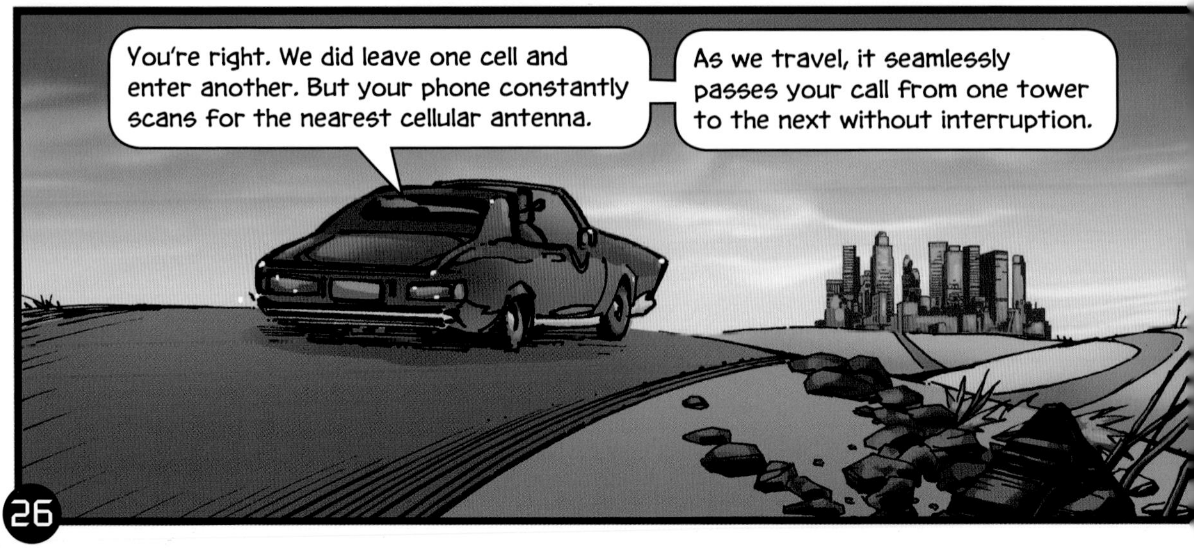
You're right. We did leave one cell and enter another. But your phone constantly scans for the nearest cellular antenna.
As we travel, it seamlessly passes your call from one tower to the next without interruption.

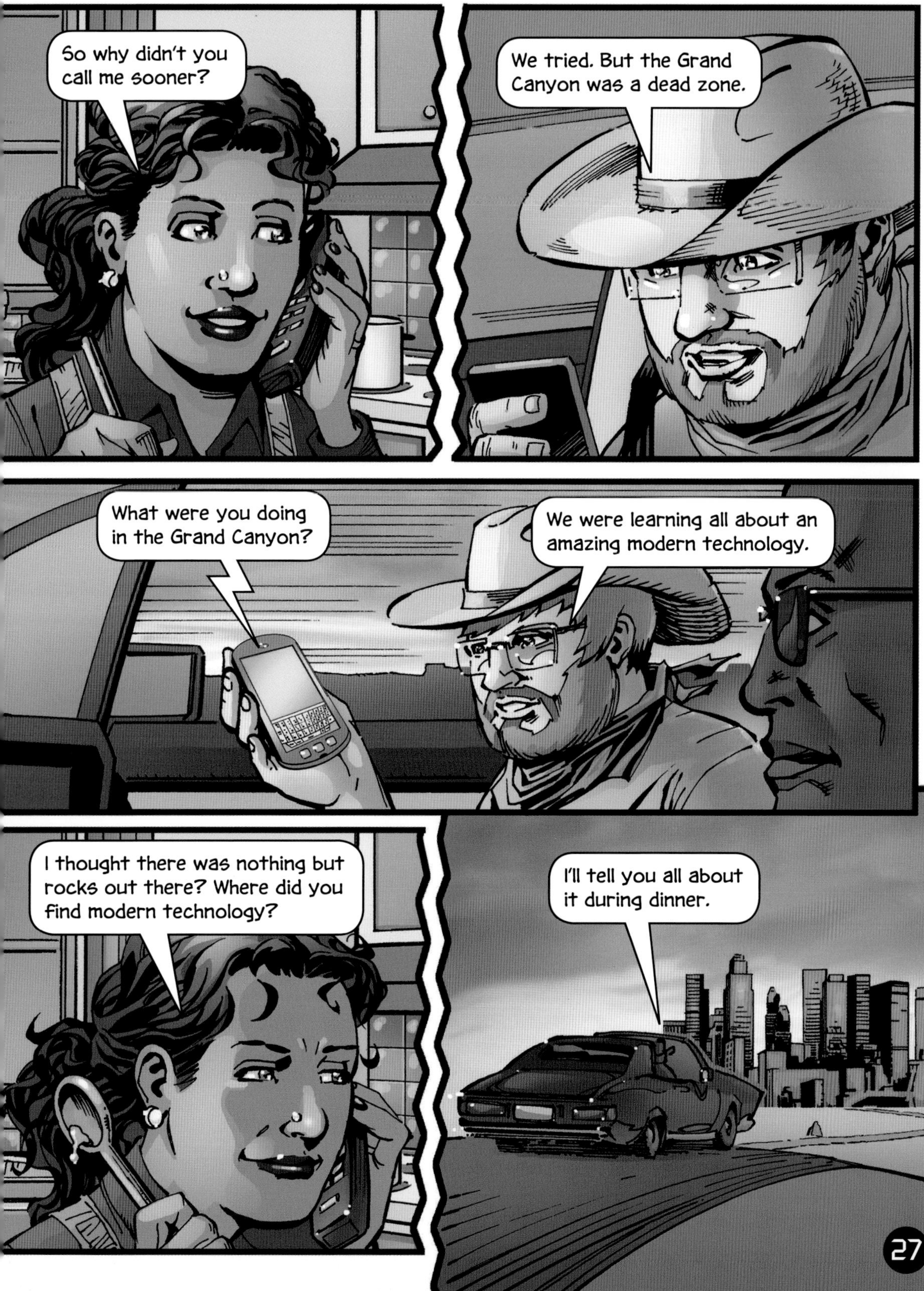
So why didn't you call me sooner?
We tried. But the Grand Canyon was a dead zone.
What were you doing in the Grand Canyon?
We were learning all about an amazing modern technology.
I thought there was nothing but rocks out there? Where did you find modern technology?
I'll tell you all about it during dinner.

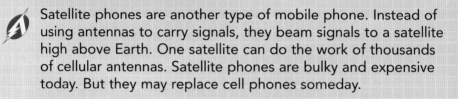

Satellite phones are another type of mobile phone. Instead of using antennas to carry signals, they beam signals to a satellite high above Earth. One satellite can do the work of thousands of cellular antennas. Satellite phones are bulky and expensive today. But they may replace cell phones someday.

Are cell phones hazardous to your health? Electromagnetic radiation is produced by the waves used to send cell phone messages. This radiation affects electrical activity in the brain. Some researchers suspect, but have yet to prove, that this radiation can cause cancer in the ears and brain.

The first successful cell phone was invented by Motorola in 1973. Early cell phones were neither small nor cheap. They were the size of a brick and sold for nearly $4,000!

New ways to use a cell phone are constantly being engineered. Most cell phone users can access the Internet and take pictures with their phones. Engineers are now working on air writing. This technology will allow people to write words in the air with their phone. The words will then show up on the cell phone's screen.

The touch screen on a cell phone is an amazing technology. Some touch screens respond to the electrical currents in your finger. Others detect the location of your touch by noticing the interruption your finger causes in sound waves or visible light.

CRITICAL THINKING USING THE COMMON CORE

1. What type of energy waves do cell phones use to make calls? Compare the characteristics of these waves to other types of energy waves in the electromagnetic spectrum. (Key Ideas and Details)

2. Why does Max display color-coded cellular grids on page 17? Explain how these illustrations help you understand the way frequencies are used in a city's cellular grid. (Craft and Structure)

3. What three codes does a cell phone always transmit when it is turned on? Explain why these codes are important to cell phone companies. (Integration of Knowledge)

MORE ABOUT

SUPER SCIENTIST

Real name: Maxwell J. Axiom
Hometown: Seattle, Washington
Height: 6' 1"   Weight: 192 lbs
Eyes: Brown   Hair: None

Super capabilities: Super intelligence; able to shrink to the size of an atom; sunglasses give x-ray vision; lab coat allows for travel through time and space.

Origin: Since birth, Max Axiom seemed destined for greatness. His mother, a marine biologist, taught her son about the mysteries of the sea. His father, a nuclear physicist and volunteer park ranger, schooled Max on the wonders of earth and sky.

One day on a wilderness hike, a megacharged lightning bolt struck Max with blinding fury. When he awoke, Max discovered a newfound energy and set out to learn as much about science as possible. He traveled the globe earning degrees in every aspect of the field. Upon his return, he was ready to share his knowledge and new identity with the world. He had become Max Axiom, Super Scientist.

antenna (an-TEN-uh)—a wire or dish that sends or receives radio waves

duplex (DOO-pleks)—having two parts

electromagnetic spectrum (i-lek-troh-mag-NET-ic SPEK-truhm)—the wide range of energy given off by the sun

engineer (en-juh-NEER)—someone trained to design and build machines, vehicles, bridges, roads, or other structures

frequency (FREE-kwuhn-see)—the number of sound waves that pass a location in a certain amount of time

grid (GRID)—a pattern of evenly spaced, or parallel, lines that cross

hertz (HURTS)—a unit for measuring the frequency of vibrations and waves; one hertz equals one wave per second

radiation (ray-dee-AY-shuhn)—rays of energy given off by certain elements

radio wave (RAY-dee-oh WAYV)—a type of electromagnetic wave; electromagnetic waves are caused by electricity and magnetism

region (REE-juhn)—a large area

rural (RUR-uhl)—of the countryside; away from cities and towns

satellite (SAT-uh-lite)—a spacecraft used to send signals and information from one place to another

simplex (SIM-pleks)—having one part

READ MORE

Bozzo, Linda. *Staying in Touch in the Past, Present, and Future.* Imagining the Future. Berkley Heights, N.J.: Enslow Publishers, 2011.

Enz, Tammy. *Zoom It: Invent New Machines that Move.* Invent It. Mankato, Minn. Capstone Press, 2012.

Hantula, Richard. *How Do Cell Phones Work?* Science in the Real World. New York: Chelsea Clubhouse, 2009.

Higgins, Nadia. *How Cell Phones Work.* Mankato, Minn.: Child's World, 2012.

McLeese, Don. *Cell Phones.* Let's Explore Technology Communications. Vero Beach, Fla.: Rourke Pub., 2009.

INTERNET SITES

FactHound offers a safe, fun way to find Internet sites related to this book. All sites on FactHound have been researched by our staff.

Here's all you do:

Visit *www.facthound.com*

Type in this code: 9781476501376

Super-cool stuff! Check out projects, games and lots more at
www.capstonekids.com

INDEX